Praise for Ken Wilcox's *Leading Through Culture*

"This excellent, insightful book ex[...] organizational culture and leadership. It's [...] lfetime
of executive accomplishments as w[...] nature.
Ken Wilcox offers readers a rare treat [...] combined with a
scholarly grasp of the subject matter. [...] both a practitioner and a theorist,
and the book reflects these two attributes. My undergraduate, graduate, and
executive students have found it extremely valuable, as have I."

> —Daniel J. Julius, visiting fellow, SOMRES research and teaching unit,
> Yale University School of Management

"Leadership is like running a restaurant: it sounds easier than it is, and everyone thinks they can do it without thinking. Ken Wilcox's book is the most
straightforward explanation I've seen that leadership is exercised through the
culture you create and how exactly you create that culture. We all may not be
able to run a successful restaurant, but we all are able to step into a leadership
role by understanding the tenets of this book."

> —Felda Hardymon, professor of management practice (retired),
> Harvard Business School; general partner, Bessemer Venture Partners

"This thoughtful, step-by-step guide to effective leadership makes a compelling case that there is nothing more fundamental to the success of any organization than its culture. Having watched Silicon Valley Bank evolve over more
than 20 years, I know that Ken Wilcox got it right. The author shares his process and the lessons he learned along the way, including his transition to an
outstanding successor. His humility and his admission to a variety of missteps
sets this book apart. I wish that every CEO and all those who aspire to lead
would read this book. I am certain that they will be enriched."

> —Pete Hart, former chairman, Silicon Valley Bank; former CEO, Advanta;
> former CEO, MasterCard International; etc.

"A gift to readers and leaders alike. Ken unwraps valuable culture change
insights through engaging storytelling, simplicity, and humor. This book is
a must-read for leaders, seasoned or aspiring, who desire to positively impact
their own organizations."

> —Sheri Benson, business counselor,
> Iowa State University SBDC, Ivy College of Business

"Ken brings an academic's discipline to bear, but more importantly, a depth of
understanding grounded in real-life interpersonal dust-ups."

> —Dave Fischer, managing partner, Gold Hill Capital

"A playbook on how to build winning teams... and how not to. Ken writes from the authority of being the CEO of one of Silicon Valley's most admired institutions. Chock-full of sage and practical advice, this book is a page-turner—which is almost unheard of in the genre of management books. A must-read for anybody leading an organization."

—Michael Moe, CEO and founder, GSV;
author, *Finding the Next Starbucks* and *The Mission Corporation*

"Ken knows how to turn a phrase with great historical and cultural context to show time-tested principles of leadership while navigating a multicultural landscape."

—Zoot Velasco, director, Gianneschi Center for Nonprofit Research,
California State University Fullerton College of Business and Economics

"I was shocked to read Ken's book because almost everything he wrote about managing a bank in America, I experienced when growing a business in China. In Ken's pages, any entrepreneur—past or present, aspiring or accomplished—will find echoes that relate directly to their professional life. Ken's book is the perfect companion to leaders of any shape or form, reminding you that you are not alone, and showing how to lead by example and from the heart to serve the needs of others.

Warning: Do not read before going to bed—you won't be able to put it down!"

—Mei Zhang, founder, WildChina

"This book brought back many fond memories I had of working with Ken over many years. I continue to utilize many of the culture and leadership principles Ken describes and, although biased, feel they're best practices. An engaging, funny, direct, and thoughtful read."

—Greg Becker, CEO, Silicon Valley Bank

"Using a combination of time-tested leadership principles and insights from the field, Ken Wilcox shows how to lead change in a cross-cultural environment, drive innovation, and deliver results. It's a must-read for anyone responsible for a team's performance."

—Ejaj Ahmad, president and founder,
Bangladesh Youth Leadership Center

"Ken's powerful insight on good leaders being focused on the welfare of their people is critical to how we lead at Oakland University."

—Michael Mazzeo, dean,
Oakland University School of Business Administration

"Ken Wilcox shares his experiences leading teams to meet performance expectations by reducing his techniques to simple applications supported by leadership theory. Ken shares real examples of how leaders drive organizational culture and provides insight that can easily be put into practice. Ken's premise is spot on: strong organizational cultures are realized when team members understand their purpose, share the organization's values, and feel supported by leaders who effectively decide, motivate, communicate, and envision."

—Kristen Migliano, PhD, associate professor of leadership and management, Lynn University; founder and lead consultant, KQ Coaching

Leading Through Culture asks the hard question up front: Do you have a vision, or do you just want to be in charge? Ken Wilcox reminds us that leadership is not just a title, but a commitment to deliberate and thoughtful practices that inspire people. He calls on us to start with ourselves and model the behaviors we value and want people in our organizations to follow. The book offers practical, tested leadership fundamentals that create a 'how-to guide' for the new leader or an opportunity for self-reflection for the experienced leader. In today's complex and constantly changing world, I value the common sense approach outlined in this book and have been sharing it with other leaders."

—Stacy M. Pell, head of employee pandemic response, Human Resources, Silicon Valley Bank

"A positive organizational culture is important in normal times. In tougher times, keeping your team together and inspired is even more crucial. I highly recommend *Leading Through Culture*. Every new founder or CEO should read this book as a prerequisite to taking investor dollars."

—Arman Zand, lecturer, Haas School of Business, University of California, Berkeley; CFO, Prodigy

"Reading and frequent reference to *Leading Through Culture* is like a rich conversation with Ken. You come away with clear, practical, and actionable recommendations. The organizational culture you create will ALWAYS trump your strategy."

—Glen Simmons, former head of Human Resources, Silicon Valley Bank, REI, etc.

"Ken Wilcox gets right to the heart of the matter: leadership is not for everyone. From the very first chapter, Wilcox challenges the reader with a series of tough, direct questions: Do you have a vision, or do you just like to be in charge? Are you skilled in communicating your vision in a way that really inspires people and captures their imagination? And, perhaps most importantly, do you genuinely care about the people you are leading? If you pass this leadership litmus test, then you will find *Leading Through Culture* an incredibly powerful—and practical—resource for building your own winning company culture. I highly recommend this book to all aspiring leaders and especially to entrepreneurs building their first company."

—Michael Dunne, CEO, ZoZoGo LLC;
author, *American Wheels, Chinese Roads;* creator, Winning In Asia Podcast

"[This] book is different from the rest because its priorities are different. Vastly different and a great deal more meaningful.... [Ken Wilcox] reminds the reader that kindness is a wonderful and desirable instrument for building up a workplace network. That winning comes from lifting up others and forming trust among colleagues. That it doesn't have to be the stereotype of dog eat dog. That you can be human and share the process with others."

—Robert Buccellato, San Francisco Book Review

"The author draws liberally on his own experiences, citing numerous examples of what to do and, perhaps more importantly, what not to do. Much of his advice is specific and actionable; for instance, he provides six recommendations for what kind of people to hire, engages in a captivating discussion about "the spectrum of human behavior," enumerates "The Magic 12" (a list of 12 ways to cultivate trust), and shares "The Four Ds," a useful process for making decisions.

Part 3 of the book, "Accomplishing Great Things: Revolutionary Leadership," is a journey into more ambitious, cutting-edge goals. A chapter on managing change demonstrates the author's deep understanding of organizational behavior.... Wilcox's perceptive observations about building a "shared culture" should prove invaluable to any leader who has global responsibilities. Throughout the book, he looks back over his senior executive experience with a critical eye, unafraid to reveal his own shortcomings. That, writes the author, is exactly what a great leader should do."

—Kirkus Reviews

LEADING
THROUGH
CULTURE

LEADING
THROUGH
CULTURE

HOW REAL LEADERS CREATE
CULTURES THAT MOTIVATE PEOPLE
TO ACHIEVE GREAT THINGS

KEN WILCOX

Waterside Productions
Cardiff-by-the-Sea, CA

Printed in the United States of America

First Printing, 2020

ISBN-13: 978-1-949003-35-2 print edition
ISBN-13: 978-1-949003-36-9 ebook edition

Waterside Productions
2055 Oxford Ave.
Cardiff-by-the-Sea, CA 92007
www.waterside.com

I DEDICATE THIS BOOK TO MY DAD.

His vision of employees self-actualizing within the context
of life in a corporation presented to me an ideal
that I would strive to help others achieve.

His patience and wisdom created a wonderful
environment for me to grow as a person
and, ultimately, as a leader.

ACKNOWLEDGMENTS

I would like to thank the people who had the patience and stamina to read, critically, and then to reread, even more critically, this manuscript: first and foremost, Kristen Garabedian, whose editorial skills have greatly enriched this book; and Ben Harrison, who created the illustrations.

I'd also like to thank the many friends who read various versions and gave me their forthright feedback along the way, including Sheila Melvin, case writer at the Stanford Graduate School of Business; Professor "Huggy" Rao, professor at the Stanford Graduate School of Business; Arman Zand, banker, entrepreneur, and teacher (at Berkeley); Grace Gardner, engagement manager, Entangled Solutions; Lewis Schlossinger, professor, Fordham University; Glen Simmons, formerly head of Human Resources at Silicon Valley Bank (SVB); and finally, Felda Hardymon, general partner at Bessemer Venture Partners and professor (retired) at the Harvard Business School; and a whole host of others.

I would also like to acknowledge three authors for the extent to which their thinking inspired mine. First, Cyrus the Great (King of

Persia, born 601 BCE, died 530 BCE). Whether or not he actually said (or wrote) "Diversity in counsel, unity in command" is irrelevant. Those words are attributed to him. And those words have had a more profound effect on my thinking than those of anyone else (except, perhaps, my dad). Second, Stephen M. R. Covey, author of *The Speed of Trust*. For years, we used his book as a basic text in our management training program at Silicon Valley Bank (SVB). Third, Patrick Lencioni (management consultant and author of more than ten books on how to run a company). He coached me in the first year or two of my tenure as CEO.

Finally, I would like to mention that many of the illustrative examples given in this book are based on the experiences I had during my thirty years at SVB. I have altered the facts to fit the point I was trying to make and changed the names to maintain anonymity.

CONTENTS

PART ONE
Should *You* Become a Leader?

CHAPTER 1

PART TWO
The Fundamentals of Leading:
Basic Techniques and Maneuvers

CHAPTER 2

CHAPTER 3
Building a Great Culture: Care About Me, Help Me Grow,

CHAPTER 4

CHAPTER 5

CHAPTER 6
Communicating with Your Constituencies:

PART THREE

Accomplishing Great Things:
Revolutionary Leadership

INTRODUCTION

I Wrote This Book to Help Others Become Good Leaders

A couple of months ago, I got an email from my friend Arman. I've known Arman for almost twenty years. I joined Silicon Valley Bank (SVB) in 1990 when I was forty-two. He joined us in early 2000, right out of college. SVB was small enough at that time that I knew almost everyone by name, including Arman. He's not easy to overlook, as his personality is "bigger than life." Given our mutual interest in foreign cultures, our paths often crossed—in India, Israel, the UK, and then later in China, where we worked together for a number of years.

"I need your advice," he wrote. "Can we meet for coffee?"

A couple of days later, we met at a Starbucks in San Francisco's South of Market (SoMA) district, today home to a very large number of start-ups. "I've just joined another start-up," he said, "called Farmstead. Think of it as a modern-day Webvan, this time driven by software and artificial intelligence. This one has a real chance of succeeding," he insisted, "but I need your help. The founders are amazing, and the technology works! It's a very young company, so we have an opportunity to build a really strong culture early. I want to get everyone to see the big picture and to motivate our team with a greater sense of purpose. Like we did at SVB! We're open to new ideas. What I really need to make this work is your book."

I'd given him an earlier draft a couple of months before. My book, the one you are just starting to read right now, is about leading a company, largely through building a culture that motivates people. Arman's message to me was simple: Finish the book and get it into print where people can use it, as quickly as possible!

———

It was April 2001, and I was about to become CEO of SVB—just in time for the worst recession in the history of American technology. For my entire eighteen-year banking career, I'd been lending money exclusively to venture-backed technology companies. I loved working with them, and as a manager for eleven years at SVB—the leading bank in this field—it was exciting to help "make the world a better place" by supporting organizations that were advancing innovation worldwide. But I wanted to do more than just provide banking services to these companies. I felt I had a unique vision of where we could take SVB to provide the most benefit to our constituencies (including shareholders, employees, customers, and the community). I really wanted to be CEO.

So, when our board asked me, I gladly accepted. At first, being "in charge" was a thrill I'd always dreamed of. That said, it wasn't clear to me that I was actually prepared to lead. Others saw this, too. In fact, one of my best friends in our industry called to say he was as thrilled as I was to hear that our board had picked the "least" likely candidate for the job. To make matters worse, our industry—and with it, our bank's results—started plummeting shortly after I took over.

It was the worst of times. Economists have since established that the great recession of 2001 started almost exactly when I became

CEO: the first quarter of 2001. First, the so-called dot-coms came crashing down, soon followed by the communications companies, and then by virtually all other tech companies. Each quarter was worse than the last. All the tech companies were running out of cash, so they had less and less money to deposit in our bank. Without deposits, we couldn't make loans. Our business, and with it our balance sheet, began to shrink. As a result, every board meeting was torture. The board members understood our plight, but as the board of a publicly traded company, they felt they had to demand results. In that era, one of our board members coined the phrase: "If the CEO enjoyed the board meeting, it wasn't a good board meeting." Well, for a number of quarters (it felt like a number of years), we never had a bad board meeting.

A graphic depicting my ten years as CEO would basically look like a valley between two mountain ranges. The CEO before me had benefited from the tech boom of the 1990s, as well as from normal to higher-than-normal interest rates. The CEO after me benefited from the tech boom of the post-2008 recession, as well as from climbing interest rates. For the entirety of my tenure as CEO, tech was in the doldrums and interest rates were among the lowest in the history of the Fed. Our business model thrives on a vibrant tech sector, and—for us—the higher the interest rates, the better. The board, while supportive, was anxious and impatient. The Fed (our regulator) was demanding. And Wall Street was critical of everything we did. First and foremost, my job was to lead our troops for an entire decade through the valley defined by the end of the dot-com boom (2001) and the beginning of the next tech boom (2011), and to keep them motivated.

To be completely honest, I was lost. At least, at first.

Over the next few challenging years, I found I had a lot to learn about leading a team through tough times. Neither my past experience nor my predecessors' examples held the answers. Solutions were not innate or intuitive.

I looked to my past for role models. Started reading. Got a coach. Talked with trusted advisors. Eventually, I found my "sea legs."

Within a few (very long) years, valued constituencies, including the board, Wall Street, clients, and employees, began praising my work.

Reflecting on those years today, I know that Vince Lombardi was right: "Leaders are not born, they are made."[1] Circumstance, not destiny, usually thrusts people into leadership roles; and they grow as leaders through advice from others, trial and error, intelligence and good sense, hard work, and resilience. Mostly, effective leadership is not innate. We have to learn it.

I realize now that I wasn't totally unprepared for this assignment. In many ways, I'd been preparing for it for years.

———

In the summer of 2008, I received an invitation to give a speech at Stanford. I love giving speeches, so I accepted, without asking too many questions. When I arrived, the arrangers handed me a form, giving Stanford the right to turn my speech into a podcast. I had no objection, as at the time I didn't really know what that meant. The capstone of my speech was the sentence: "Culture trumps strategy." And that is how I obtained my proverbial fifteen minutes of fame. This is likely the only sentence I've ever uttered that people will quote.[2]

Shortly after that speech at Stanford, I started writing this book, on weekends and during vacations. Why? Because I'd started my journey almost eight years before, with very few positive role models to follow. My prior bosses had serious flaws, I thought, and as I looked around me at the world at large, I couldn't find very many others I wanted to copy. To find the answers I was looking for, I'd had to turn to history and to my own trial-and-error experience as CEO for the eight years prior. As I look around me today, I do not

1   Vince Lombardi, "Famous Quotes by Vince Lombardi," VinceLombardi.com, accessed April 9, 2018, http://www.vincelombardi.com/quotes.html.

2   In 2013, two other authors (Curt Coffman and Kathie Sorenson) came out with a book entitled *Culture Eats Strategy for Lunch: The Secret of Extraordinary Results.* They attribute the first half of their title to Peter Drucker. Apparently, I am not the first to have noted that culture is much more important than strategy.

believe that the situation has improved a lot. Think about the examples we read about in the press today:

→ "Trump Destroys American Greatness from Within," *New York Times*, June 7, 2019

→ "A number of current and former Wells Fargo employees tell the *New York Times* that contrary to the company's promises, its culture remains troubled," *Barron's*, March 11, 2019

→ "Uber: The Scandals that Drove Travis Kalanick out," *BBC News*, June 21, 2017

→ "Mark Zuckerberg Lied to Congress about Facebook Data Scandal, Congressman Claims," *The Independent*, June 5, 2018

→ "Theranos Founder Elizabeth Holmes Charged with Massive Fraud," *CNN Money*, March 14, 2018

So, what about books on leadership? Aren't there enough of them out there already?

Yes, leadership books are legion, but most suffer from one or more of the following:

1. **Too theoretical:** The author may know a lot but hasn't practiced much.

2. **Too practical:** The author offers suggestions through anecdotes but is light on principles. What are the reasons behind the author's good advice, anyway?

3. **Too focused on winning:** Many leadership books are about how to win, in the market or inside the company, by beating out competitors.

4. **Too focused on making a splash:** Often designed for people who have just replaced a leader, such books invariably advise observing for one hundred days, then dramatically coming out with a major-league, watershed program that turns everything upside-down and demonstrates beyond any doubt one's leadership prowess.

5. **Too focused on the leader's personality:** These books describe who should, based on innate personality, be a leader. Unfortunately, this precludes many of us from even considering a leadership role.

6. **Too focused on the personality of a single leader who led a single company, that—at the moment— most consider successful:** These include the various books about Jack Welch, Steve Jobs, etc. Such books often seem to imply a direct cause-effect relationship between the particular leader's personality and his/her company's apparent success.

7. **Too trendy:** I recently read *Bad Blood* by John Carreyrou, the story of Theranos, the blood-testing company founded by Elizabeth Holmes. Theranos will go down in history as one of Silicon Valley's most interesting and most dramatic failures. The founder and CEO, Elizabeth Holmes, deliberately modeled herself after Steve Jobs, as presented by Walter Isaacson in his famous biography. Sadly, it would appear that she most admired many of Jobs' worst tendencies: humiliating others in public, obsession with secrecy, tyrannical outbursts, etc. When I read Isaacson's book, my most immediate response was fear that young, ambitious entrepreneurs like Holmes would mistakenly conclude that it was these tendencies that led to Apple's success.

Why is *Leading Through Culture* different? Because real life generally differs in the following ways:

1. **Successful leadership is based on a collaborative style.** Most of history's best leadership examples are collaborative, not dictatorial. Over time, a confidence-inspiring leadership team invariably accomplishes more, with better results, than one charismatic (and often tyrannical) leader.

2. **Most books base their accolades on a single constituency's satisfaction.** If Wall Street is happy, for instance, then the leader must have done a good job and is, therefore, by definition, a great leader. In my view, good leadership seeks to optimize the experience for all of a group's significant constituencies. It's nice if Wall Street is happy, but we don't have an example of good leadership unless other major constituencies (employees, clients, the community, regulators, etc.) are happy, too.

3. **Most books on leadership seem to be about making more money or improving the bottom line.** Success isn't just about money. It's also about happiness. If all constituencies are happy over time, there will be money— perhaps more than there might be otherwise.

4. **This book is intended as a "field manual." It is practical.** It starts with the question: "Why do you want to lead?" and helps you answer it for yourself. From that point on, it is organized in a logical, sequential way, in the order in which things actually develop in real life: building a team, creating a culture, getting everyone pointed in the right direction, how to work together on a daily basis with your leadership team, how you and your leadership team can work effectively with the organization as a whole, etc.

5. **Finally, my approach to writing.** For active leaders, a book must be short. I hope and believe I've achieved that.

6. **My approach sounds simple, but it is much more difficult than it appears.** I'll bet you'll agree: Many of the most obvious leadership principles at least appear to have been ignored by the leaders you have experienced in your lives. If a principle is so obvious that it appears simple, and still is ignored by most leaders, to their detriment, then in my view it bears discussion. This may result in parts of my manual seeming simple. Believe me, even the simple things are difficult. Otherwise, why would leaders so often fail to practice them?

This book's basic principles apply to leaders across a wide variety of organization types and sizes. Silicon Valley Bank was a start-up when I joined it in 1990. It had about 1,200 people in total when I passed my CEO baton on to my successor, Greg Becker, ten years later; today, under Greg's leadership, it is one of the largest banks in the US and one of only a handful with a global orientation. And yet, I believe that the stories and principles elucidated in the book apply to every part of this journey from start-up to global bank. In addition, I wrote this book with leaders of all kinds of organizations in mind, not just CEOs of corporations, but rather *anyone* who finds themselves in positions of leadership. This includes department heads, scout leaders, heads of not-for-profits, work group leaders, church leaders, school principals, etc. Literally *all those* who find themselves in a position of leadership, for whatever timeframe, at whatever stage of an organization's development.

Leading Through Culture will guide you through many aspects of leadership, in three parts.

In Part One, we'll focus on leaders as people and explore the unique aspects of their relationships with others. Any of us may be called to lead, for a short time or a longer one, in a large or small group, and almost all of us are capable. Here, you'll learn the two most important aspects of leadership: 1) leading by example, and 2) serving the needs of others.

In Part Two, we'll examine leadership: what to do, how to do it, and how to build and work with a leadership team, since effective leaders accomplish much more through others than they do alone. We'll take a look at culture. Every group has a culture, and some work better than others, so how do you create an optimal one? How do you get your leadership team all pointed in the same direction? And, having set a direction, how do you get your team working together to get the job done? Finally, what are the best ways to communicate with various constituencies? Getting the job done is one thing, but failing to communicate it effectively is actually quite another. Here you'll learn techniques for effective communication, which is key to ultimate success.

In Part Three, we'll explore leadership at its highest level. How do you effect change, create an environment that encourages real innovation, and lead in a cross-cultural environment? How can you make a difference that affects the future, not just the present? Here we'll examine strategies for "making the world a better place."

———

In retrospect, I owe my dad a debt of gratitude. He was a pretty unusual guy. While other dads where I grew up in Michigan spent their father/son time in the backyard tossing footballs, or out in the field hunting pheasants, my dad was editing our (I was one of three brothers) essays, coaching us in public speaking, and lecturing us around the dining room table about organizational behavior.

My dad worked as a teacher at General Motors Institute in Flint, Michigan—the only automotive engineering school in the world at that time, in the only department not involved in some aspect of engineering (initially, public speaking and technical writing; and later on, organizational behavior). He believed that corporations, while necessary, were unnatural to the point of toxicity. In his experience, most corporate employees disliked coming to work in the morning. Impressed by Maslow's concept of the hierarchy of needs (self-actualization being the highest level), my dad believed that everyone wanted most to self-actualize and that corporations were not designed to foster this. But they *could* be, he argued. If and when they changed in that way, productivity levels and therefore profits would be greater than ever. My dad dreamed of a day when people would leap out of bed in the morning filled with enthusiasm and joyfully participate in the corporation's work. In so doing, they would fully realize their potential as human beings *and* contribute to the corporation's success.

I hope and believe that leaders who adopt the practices in this book will create a culture that makes people feel the way my dad dreamed things could be. None of this information comes directly from my dad, but it's heavily influenced by his way of thinking. My dad and his ideas inspire me daily. For all he did and all he was, I am forever grateful. What he taught me, overtly and by example, helped me steer the ship during my years at the helm of SVB.

Another unlikely influence was my ninth-grade English teacher, Paul Whiteman, who taught at the middle school I attended in Flint, Michigan. He taught English, and his wife taught Latin. They were easily the two most sophisticated teachers in the entire school. Every year at the ninth-grade prom, Mr. and Mrs. Whiteman waited on the sideline for the real ballroom music, played occasionally between runs of '60s rock, to show us all how it looked to be elegant (following which, they escaped to Europe for the summer to recharge their batteries and prepare for fall).

Among other things, Mr. Whiteman made us memorize poems. He selected poems based on what they taught us about how to lead our lives. One (by R. L. Sharpe) in particular has stuck in my head for all these years:

Isn't it strange
That princes and kings,
And clowns that caper
In sawdust rings,
And common people
Like you and me
Are builders for eternity?
Each is given a bag of tools,
A shapeless mass,
A book of rules;
And each must make—
Ere life is flown—
A stumbling block
Or a stepping stone.[3]

Real leaders, in the eyes of both my dad and Mr. Whiteman, care about others. Their goal in leading is neither power, nor money, nor self-aggrandizement. Their goal is leaving behind a better place for all.

---

3   R. L. Sharpe, "A Bag of Tools," Poetry Nook, accessed April 10, 2018, https://www.poetrynook.com/poem/bag-tools.

PART ONE

SHOULD *YOU* BECOME A LEADER?

CHAPTER 1

WHY DO YOU WANT TO LEAD?

Xi Baba and The Donald

What this chapter is all about:

In this first part of the book, we talk about becoming a leader. If you want to lead, what are some of the things you should be thinking about? Here are some of the questions you might want to answer:

- Do you have a vision, or do you just like the idea of being in charge?

- Do you know your strengths and weaknesses?

- Are you prepared to work on your weaknesses for as long as it takes?

- Are you prepared to deal with the fact that, as a leader, people will be copying your behavior, all day long?

- Do you want to become a master of your trade or a leader of masters?

- Are you prepared to truly leverage yourself through others?

One day in 1989, I was having lunch with the then-head of 3I (Investors in Industry, a British private equity firm) at the Méridien Hotel in Boston, Bill Holmes. I was a vice president at the well-respected Bank of New England. We were the market leaders (in New England, *not* in California) in lending money to early-stage technology companies. And I was the most experienced member of the subgroup that focused on raw start-ups. I really liked what I did. I was getting recognition from others, both in the bank and in the market. Bill asked me if I liked my job. I told him that life was "as good as it gets."

Only a few months later, the real estate recession migrated from Texas to New England. The federal regulators migrated with it, and they were loaded for bear.

By the end of 1989, it was apparent that the Bank of New England (BNE) was on its way into receivership. In April of 1990, the core of our little tech lending team left BNE to join Silicon Valley Bank, forming its first office outside of Silicon Valley, on Route 128! We were all proud of our bold move and happy to be part of a very cool new bank, focused primarily on lending to tech companies.

Within a matter of months, the real estate recession that had afflicted first Texas and then New England moved on to California. Although our new home, Silicon Valley Bank, was building its reputation on lending to tech companies, behind the scenes, a large part of our revenues derived from loans to small real estate developers. Soon, Silicon Valley Bank was in trouble as well. The head of our new office on 128 (i.e., my boss) was called to Silicon Valley to help save the bank from going under. Soon, our bank had a brand-new turnaround CEO, and my former boss left the organization, leaving me in charge of our activities in New England.

Gradually, my life changed. Instead of building a portfolio of tech companies, I found myself building a team of tech lenders. I was confronted with a whole new set of challenges, and I was finding that I liked it even more than what I'd done before. This was my chance to make things better. I'd never felt that any of my previous bosses had done that good of a job, of either building the kind of infrastructure that would enable us to help our clients succeed, or of creating the kind of environment that would encourage us to support each other for our collective benefit. Now, for the first time, I could do something about it. If life was "as good as it gets" before, it was *even better* now. If I really liked what I did before, I really loved it now. Our little office on Route 128 grew fast, both in headcount and in client base. Soon, we were viewed within the bank as one of the most exciting and fulfilling places to work.

By 1995, our new CEO, the "turnaround guy," had accomplished his mission. Silicon Valley Bank was back on track. People were wondering how long he would stay on. When would we be getting another new CEO? Who might that person be? Who *in* the bank might qualify? A few of my closest colleagues started asking me if I would be interested if the opportunity were to present itself.

Circumstances forced me to think about it. By throwing my hat in the ring, I had nothing to lose. On the other hand, if I didn't, and the board brought in someone else, that new person might not grant me the same level of autonomy to build what I already had begun to think of as "my half of the country": everything east of the Mississippi. I might have to "toe the line" and accept a completely different set of approaches, in effect undoing all the improvements I had implemented. I had a vision of where I wanted to take "my bank," and I didn't want to relinquish my opportunity to lead us there. To be clear, it wasn't so much that I really wanted to be in charge; it was more that I didn't want anyone else to be. If someone else took over, they might not have a vision at all (it wasn't apparent to me that the CEOs I'd experienced before had had one), and even if they did, it might not be one I'd want to be led to.

This was the first in a series of questions that the new set of circumstances forced me over time to ask myself. In these next few pages, I would like to walk you through the most important ones.

DO YOU HAVE A VISION, OR DO YOU JUST WANT TO BE IN CHARGE?

The first, and in many respects most important question, I believe, is this: What makes you tick? What is your primary motivation? Why do you want to lead?

In my experience, there are fundamentally two possible motivations for becoming a leader: 1) the desire for power or control, and 2) the desire to do something good. Of course, almost any leader has a mix of these two. But, in most cases, it's pretty easy to tell which motivation is primary and which is secondary.

The internet is packed with quotes attributed to famous people. I don't know if Helen Keller—a remarkable visionary with one of the most resilient spirits in history—*actually* said this, but I was so struck by it that I want to share it with you: "The only thing worse than being blind is having sight but no vision."[4]

If you have a vision—if you know what you'd like to accomplish, where you'd like your followers to go, what you'd like them to do to get there, why they should go there, what it will be like for them once they arrive, and why they, as well as their constituencies, will all be better off for it—and if your primary motivation for getting power or control is to make your vision a reality, all other factors being equal, your followers will be drawn to you and will want to follow you.

On the other hand, if your primary motivation is power and control, few will be drawn to you and few will follow.

We all know leaders who fit into each of these two categories. In the latter, we often find people who are bossy and self-centered, who are self-serving and self-aggrandizing, who hold the people working for them to one standard and themselves to another. One clear sign: if it's unclear what their goals are, or if their goals seem to shift in response to public sentiment, it could be that they really don't have a vision—at least not one that goes beyond being in charge.

---

4   Attributed to Helen Keller, "Helen Keller Quotes," BrainyQuote, accessed June 3, 2021, https://www.brainyquote.com/quotes/helen_keller_383771.

On the other hand, most of our best-known and most admired leaders clearly had a vision: George Washington, Abraham Lincoln, Mahatma Gandhi, etc. Washington, a reluctant leader who had to be persuaded to don the mantle of leadership, wanted most to set the fledgling country on a right course. For him, that meant governing in a way that did not take the country in the direction of reestablishing a kingdom. He had just finished fighting a long and difficult war to free the country from being governed by a king, a monarch whose primary motivation for governing was simply that he was next in a hereditary line that symbolized power (far more than a vision or program). It appears to me that Lincoln wanted to be president so that he would have the power to keep the Union together and also to solve the problem of slavery. Gandhi wasn't even looking for power. More than anything, he wanted to free India from British rule and help Indians improve their lives, and he did his best to influence events in a way that would enable him to realize his vision.

I am writing these sentences in 2020. The two most powerful countries in the world today are led by Xi Jin Ping (often referred to in the Chinese press as *Xi Baba* or "Daddy Xi") and Donald Trump ("The Donald"), respectively. It is interesting to think about this issue ("visionary" or "power-hungry narcissist") in relation to these two larger-than-life leaders. Do they each have a vision? Is it a compelling one? To what extent are they really motivated by a desire for power, and to what extent by a desire to realize their respective visions? Where are they each on the power-vision spectrum?

Over the long haul, no one can make you powerful by bestowing on you a title, nor can you make yourself powerful by obtaining one. Only you can genuinely make yourself powerful, and you can only do that by having and articulating a vision, or at least a plan of action, that inspires others to follow you. That vision, or plan, has to be one that helps your followers achieve something that they perceive as valuable.

"Remember," George Washington admonished the officers of the Virginia Regiment, "that it is the actions, and not the commission, that make the officer—and that there is more expected from him than the *title*."[5]

So, the first and I think most important question is: Do you have a vision of where you would like to take the organization you will be leading, and is that vision a compelling one for the people you will be leading? Or do you just like being in charge because you like telling other people what to do?

The second question, which we will be dealing with in the next section, is this: Do you have the right attributes? I believe that most people can learn *the principles of leadership*. That said, I do *not* think that everyone has the *right attributes* to be a good leader.

Ask yourself:

→ Do I have a "vision"?

→ Can I articulate my vision?

→ Do I willingly communicate my vision to others?

→ Am I comfortable delegating?

→ When I delegate, do I just delegate tasks, or am I willing to delegate decision-making (within parameters) as well?

→ Do I tell people what to do, or do I share a vision and ask them to join me in trying to decide what to do?

→ Why do I want to be a leader? Because I like being in charge? Or because I want to realize my vision?

→ What kinds of leaders are Xi Baba and The Donald? How would you describe them? What are their goals and motivations?

---

5   George Washington, "George Washington, January 8, 1756, General Orders," in *George Washington Papers, Series 2, Letterbooks 1754 to 1799: Letterbook 3,-Sept. 18, 1756.* 1755. Manuscript/mixed material, accessed October 14, 2018, https://www.loc.gov/item/mgw2.003/.

KNOW YOUR STRENGTHS AND WEAKNESSES

Shortly after becoming CEO of Silicon Valley Bank, I implemented a "360 process" for all of my management team members, to help us understand what we were—and weren't—doing well. Like most people, I was thinking about how this would apply to others, and not so much to myself. I knew that I had my faults; everyone does. But I was shocked to learn that some of my management team members were actually afraid of me. I felt so hurt when the consultants took me aside and revealed that several of my direct reports found me difficult to deal with. Everyone agreed that I had strong principles and that they knew what I stood for. But when a team member would voice an opinion contradicting one of my strongly held principles, I sometimes responded in a way that others viewed as harsh, even vindictive. No one wants to work with, and especially not for, an overly critical, mean-spirited person. Especially if that person doesn't even see those qualities in himself.

There are a number of personality traits that we in this day and age associate with good leaders, and I'd like to list some of them here. It's not necessary to have all of them. What *is* necessary, however, is to know what your personality traits are, which are good ones and which are perhaps not so good, and to have a willingness to work on changing or at least mitigating the impact of those that are not so good.

Read the modern literature on leadership and you'll see a heavy emphasis on the concept of "authenticity." It's important to be genuine, which means letting people know who you are, your likes and dislikes, and most important, your values. Many leaders hide behind a facade because they think that being themselves isn't enough. So they try to project an image of something they are not. They "hide," if you will, behind a mask, never letting anyone know what they really look like. They're afraid that their real self won't command sufficient respect, and that others will see them for who they really are, and that who they really are doesn't really command respect.

Yes, today's followers demand authenticity from their leaders. Real leaders have the confidence to be themselves. You can't be a phony and expect people to follow you willingly over time. Sooner or later, they'll notice the discrepancies. Nor can you hide behind a facade of being "corporate" or "religious" or "politically correct." You must allow your real self to shine through. Otherwise, people will perceive you as a fraud or tinny and stilted, or worse yet, hypocritical. Either way, they'll experience you as lacking in authenticity and won't be able to connect with you. Their desire to follow you will diminish.

To be authentic means, among other things, to be honest with yourself and with others about your strengths *and* your shortcomings. To be authentic, you must engage in genuine self-reflection, admit to your mistakes, and learn from them.

To my way of thinking, another word for "authenticity" is "vulnerability." Real leaders are vulnerable. They're willing to admit to their shortcomings and mistakes. Without this quality, no one can be a true leader.

"I am as frail a mortal as any of us and I never had anything extraordinary about me nor have any now," said Gandhi. "I claim to be a simple individual liable to err like any other fellow mortal. I own, however, that I have humility enough in me to confess my errors and to retrace my steps. . . . If we are to make progress, we must not repeat history but make new history."[6] Within our own circumstances, we can realize our leadership potential by cultivating authenticity and humility. Putting in the effort and doing our best to be ourselves, to improve, and to shore up our weaknesses, truly matters.

I recall one of my direct reports who, during the interview process, seemed to be smart, knowledgeable, and a good and genuine person. Impressed, I hired him. His first day on the job coincided with an off-site team-building exercise led by a consultant we'd been

6 Mohandas Karamchand Gandhi, in *The Essential Gandhi: An Anthology of His Writings on His Life, Work, and Ideas*, ed. Louis Fischer (New York: Vintage Books, 2002), xxvi.

using for years. This consultant knew our team well and understood the concepts I've discussed here: authenticity, vulnerability, and humility. The next day (my new employee's second day on the job), our consultant called me after work and said: "I don't mean to be discouraging, and if I turn out to be wrong I want to apologize in advance, but I think you made a mistake when you hired George, and I think that it may turn out to have been a fairly big one." Naturally, I was a bit put off. I was really proud of my "catch" and— at the same time—curious.

"What do you mean?" I asked.

"He lacks authenticity," the consultant said. "He refuses to be vulnerable."

Sadly, people in business often misinterpret vulnerability. They confuse it with weakness. Nothing could be further from the truth. *Truly confident people are willing to be vulnerable.* And, *I've never met an arrogant person who did not lack confidence.* Behind every bully I've ever met is an insecure, often frightened person.

Sure enough, our consultant was right. George's personality soon revealed itself. He was *always* right—or so he thought—and never seemed to question himself. And since he was always "right," by definition those who disagreed with him were always "wrong." Over time, George's goodness, to the extent that it was real, felt imposing and, to the extent that it wasn't, superficial.

In time, George had to leave. He did so voluntarily, but if he hadn't, he might have gotten "voted off the island." People grew to think of him as self-righteous and phony. Even as he left, he had not yet taken off his mask, either in front of others at work or—I suspect—in front of himself, as he looked in the mirror, alone, at home.

Beyond *authenticity, vulnerability, humility, and confidence,* I would list *kindness, humor, and courage* as characteristics that are desirable (and perhaps even necessary) in a leader. To succeed in his reform efforts, Mahatma Gandhi exhibited a kind of undaunted courage that allowed people to trust and follow him with confidence, never doubting how he would respond to a provocation. He never asked his followers to do anything he was unwilling to do himself, and he risked his life many times on the front lines of his efforts for peace and justice. Accordingly, his followers did as well. Ultimately, his work led to the end of British rule in India and improved the quality of life for the country's poorer classes, and his influence extended well beyond his own time. Years later, halfway around the world, Martin Luther King Jr and other civil rights leaders modeled their nonviolent resistance practices after Gandhi's example. As a role model, Gandhi continues to change the world today. He worked deliberately to set an example that would strengthen India's civil rights movement. His efforts were often noble and played out on a grand scale, and they sprang from a kind heart. But he was only human, after all, and had to deal with the same types of challenges and daily annoyances as the rest of us. Gandhi cited his sense of humor as a critical resource in dealing with some of life's more trying aspects. Just remember, as a leader you're *always* setting an example, even in the small and sometimes humorous moments that make up daily life.

A kindhearted sense of humor, which humility makes possible, can be a real asset. Consider how Abraham Lincoln used humor to gracefully exit an awkward situation. *London Times* reporter William Russell wrote at the time: "In the conversation which occurred before dinner, I was amused to observe the manner in which Mr. Lincoln used the anecdotes for which he is famous. Where men bred in courts, accustomed to the world, or versed in diplomacy, would use some subterfuge, or would make a polite speech, or give a shrug of the shoulders as the means of getting out of an embarrassing position, Mr. Lincoln raises a laugh by some bold west-country anecdote, and moves off in the cloud of merriment produced by his joke."[7]

Maintaining a sense of humor and treating others with kindness can be a saving grace in this world. Lacking these qualities

7   William Howard Russell, from "Views of President Lincoln, 1861," 2005, Eyewitness to History, accessed October 14, 2018, www.eyewitnesstohistory.com/lincoln2.htm.

can make you inaccessible, at best, and a target, at worst. Who's the guy that everyone wants to see slip on a banana peel? The bully, the stuffed shirt, the guy so full of himself that he spends his time browbeating others. People wait gleefully for that kind of person to screw up and fail. Why wouldn't you want those people on your side, instead? We all have our limitations. Recognize that you have your own healthy share and use your gifts of authenticity, humility, a gentle sense of humor, and true kindness toward others to make the best of things.

Finally, a good leader never "punches down." Make a gently self-deprecating remark as a leader, and people find you accessible. Make a joke at another's expense, particularly someone below you in rank, situation, or power, and you reveal your cruelty. Like all bullies, your weakness will be on full display.

Combine kindness and humor with the kind of courage and determination that Gandhi summoned in taking on the British Empire, and that Lincoln brought to bear in fighting to save the Union and eradicate slavery, and you have some of the essential hallmarks of true leadership.

Few people always exhibit authenticity, confidence, courage, kindness, and humor. That said, real leaders know themselves, and they are at least aware of the extent to which they exhibit these characteristics. And, to the extent that they do not exhibit them, true leaders are dedicated to becoming the best they can be. In other words, they are constantly striving to improve. The truth is, we're never really completely ready to lead, and no matter how hard we try, we never really get there. Becoming a leader is in large part a question of committing to a never-ending process.

Think of professional athletes, and how they are always working on whatever is crucial to success in their sport. I'm no golfer, but golfers always tell me that they're always working on their swing. No matter how good it gets, it's never really good enough. Even professional golfers, like Tiger Woods, are always working on their swing.

Ask yourself:

→ How authentic am I on a day-to-day basis? To what extent do I personify "what you see is what you get" in my work and private life?

→ How close am I to being "genuinely good"?

→ To what extent do I embody humility and vulnerability in my words and deeds?

→ Am I a fundamentally kind person? Am I sometimes harsh and/or vengeful, and if so, to what kinds of people and situations do I typically react in this way?

→ Do I maintain a sense of humor in the face of adversity?

→ Do I ask my team members to do anything that I would be unwilling to do myself? If so, why?

→ Am I capable of exhibiting genuine courage?

→ Am I consistently a person of integrity?

→ How do others experience me?

→ Is their view of me consistent with my view of myself?

→ What are my strengths and weaknesses?

→ Which of my weaknesses are fixable, and what can I do to fix them?

→ Am I willing to work on fixing them?

→ When am I willing to start?

ARE YOU PREPARED TO BE COPIED, EVERY DAY?

Many years ago, when our son, Nate, was two, my wife, Ruth, and I got stuck in heavy traffic heading back to Boston after a week's vacation in Maine. Nate was in the back seat of the car. As we inched along Route 1, where traffic usually raced by at sixty miles per hour, my stomach tied itself in knots as I imagined the pile of work awaiting me the next morning. Had anything terrible happened in my absence? This was before the days of cell phones and email, and when we went on vacation, we were truly out of touch. My heart was pounding. All I wanted was to get home. As we inched along in the sea of traffic, the rude drivers jockeying between lanes just made things worse.

Frustrated, I rolled down my window and offered some free advice (and seasoned words) to the driver next to me. Catharsis! I sighed in relief. Suddenly, from the mouth of our adorable toddler tucked in his car seat, came a mile-long string of obscenities. Apparently, Nate had stored up every curse word he'd overheard in his short life and somehow knew they belonged together. Here was his chance to let them fly! Shaken, I turned to Ruth: "Now where in hell do you think he learned that?!"

You probably have similar examples. Here's one from corporate life: Like all leaders, SVB's first CEO had strengths and weaknesses. His most obvious flaw? Incessant swearing. He almost seemed to pride himself on working the "F-word" at least once into every paragraph. In fact, there was a time when he would give anyone who would call him on it a dollar, just to penalize himself, to motivate himself to stop. Predictably, he never really stopped. We all followed suit. Everyone at SVB swore, whenever we felt like it. After nine years, our first CEO retired and in came the next CEO, who virtually never swore. Within weeks, the swearing stopped at SVB. It just disappeared. Was there a memo? I never saw one. We all followed our new leader's example, and our new leader didn't swear.

Another example: Our CEO hired a new Chief Credit Officer, and soon after, a new CIO. Fast friends, these proficient young men grew enamored of Warner Bros. ties. By year's end, not only were they sporting Porky Pig, Elmer Fudd, and Bugs Bunny ties on a daily basis, so were many other men at SVB. By spring, virtually every man (including myself) and even some women wore them regularly. A few years later, these two executives left us and by year's end, the Warner Bros. ties had vanished from SVB's halls. Was there a memo? I never saw one.

Whether you and your team wear Tweety Bird ties is insignificant. Swearing, at least in today's world, is something different. But what I'm saying isn't about ties or swearing. It's about imitating. Remember, the people you lead will copy you, whether they realize it or not, and whether you want them to or not. Whatever the behavior, if you don't want them to do it, don't do it yourself.

Whatever your mission and goals, this is a crucial time for self-reflection. As a leader, what do you want your legacy to be? Like it or not, people will be copying you. They're doing it whether they mean to or not, and whether they even *know* it or not. You have no control over whether people reporting to you (and those reporting to them) will copy you. They just will. If you come in early, they will come in early. If you cheat on your travel expenses, they will cheat on their travel expenses. If you show respect for others, they will, too. And they'll always remember the things you did that they copied.

Sometimes this "law of nature" extends to what seem like trivial issues, which, in the end, can take on the aura of importance. I was on the board of a well-known government entity (I won't say which) for several years. At the time, I was more-or-less addicted to looking at email on my PDA, about every five minutes. Out of decorum, I was committed, at least at the start, to breaking this habit during these board meetings. I did pretty well, for one meeting. Then I noticed that the chair of the board was often looking at his, and fiddling with the keys on his keyboard. What a relief! I wouldn't have to fight my internal demons after all, I decided. If the board chair could give in to his, I could surrender to mine, as well. So I did. Years later, I learned that he wasn't actually looking at email. He was playing video games. Knowing that, I felt totally justified in my questionable behavior.

George Washington understood the extent to which leaders are copied, and it deeply concerned him. "I walk on untrodden ground," he said. "There is scarcely an action, the motive of which may not be subject to a double interpretation. There is scarcely any part of my conduct, which may not hereafter be drawn into precedent."[8] With this awareness, he took every action—no matter how small—very seriously because he understood its potential impact. From this foundation of self-awareness, Washington established countless political and societal norms that have represented the best of American character for over two centuries. From seemingly trivial decisions, like clothing choice (would he dress like the ordinary citizens he represented, or as someone who thought himself part of the aristocracy?), to larger decisions, like setting the precedent of office term limits, Washington constantly acted in the spirit of public service, not self-enrichment. The good of the country was his top priority, and he worked to set a positive example for the American people through his words and actions. His reputation for honesty and decency created trust: the most precious quality in dealing with others. After two successful terms, with many people wanting him to serve longer, he established perhaps the greatest presidential norm of all: a graceful transfer of power and return to the honorable rank of private citizen.

On a less sublime level, here's another example. Do you remember *The Sopranos*? I recently binge-watched the entire series, compelled. In one scene, Tony is eating dinner with his "team." They're (appropriately) seated at a round table, where they can all see each other. Tony is telling jokes, which he seems to find uproariously funny. As you'd expect, all of his "team members" are howling with laughter. At this point, through clever use of the camera, the director shows the audience that Tony suddenly realizes that his

---

8 George Washington, in *The Writings of George Washington: Being His Correspondence, Addresses, Messages, and Other Papers, Official and Private, Selected and Published from the Original Manuscripts*, ed. Jared Sparks, (Boston: Russell, Shattuck, and Williams and Hilliard, Gray, and Co., 1836), 69.

lieutenants are all laughing because he's laughing. In a flash of insight, he understands that they're copying his laughter more than they're laughing at his humor. Recently, I witnessed the same phenomenon in a management meeting, at a company led by a very commanding CEO. As is more typically the case, I doubt this CEO experienced the same flash of insight that Tony had.

As a leader, you must exhibit behavior that you want others to copy. Simply put, you need to be good. If you have to be good, and at the same time authentic, logically you need to be "genuinely good." Well, very few people are genuinely good. But to be an effective leader over the long haul, you must try to be. An essential difference between people who are leaders and people who aren't is that real leaders consciously work at being genuinely good. Others see this, find it inspiring, and feel motivated to follow.

This holds tremendous implications. First, it suggests that leaders aren't born; they're made. That is, they make themselves. It also suggests that there's hope for all of us who aspire to lead. We can succeed if we're willing to do the work.

As a leader, *you must be the person that you want others to be.* Actively model the qualities you want to see in your team. Do something good, and people will follow your positive example. Do something bad—and guess what, you won't get good behavior.

Ask yourself:

→ Which of my behaviors or characteristics would I like people in my organization to copy?

→ Which of my behaviors or characteristics would I *not* like them to copy? What are some concrete steps I can take to change these behaviors in myself so that people in my organization don't start copying them?

→ What is the change I want to encourage in the organization I am about to lead?

→ As a leader, what do I want my legacy to be?

DO YOU WANT TO BE AN EXPERT OR A LEADER?

Almost all ambitious people want to be promoted. But not all of them really want to be leaders. They just want to be promoted because they want to be recognized. Unfortunately, most organizations don't seem to recognize this basic human need, or—if they do—they don't seem to take the steps necessary to accommodate it. The person who is best at a specific job (the best lender in a group of lenders, the best accountant in a group of accountants, the best salesperson in a group of salespeople) may or *may not* be the best one in the group to *lead*. Often the best person to lead is not the best one at the job itself. So, one of two things happens, neither of which is good for anybody. Either the person who is best at the job is promoted into the position of leader and they end up being a poor leader, or the person who would be the best leader is promoted, and the person who is best at the job itself feels cheated and quits. The group loses its most expert member.

At Shawmut Bank, where I started my career, we had a guy named Bill, who was far and away the best salesperson in the whole organization. I had a chance to "carry his bag" for a couple of months as a part of my apprenticeship. I marveled at his skill. That said, the bank had long since recognized that Bill was a poor manager. Selling to people and managing people are two different things. The bank recognized that and created two separate career paths for bankers, one that culminated in "professional salesperson" and a parallel one that culminated in "professional manager." They channeled Bill into the former, he received the recognition he yearned for, and everybody was better off.

At Silicon Valley Bank, at least when I first arrived, we had not yet come to that realization. The really good bankers (actually, *all* of the bankers, good or not so good) wanted to be promoted into the role of a manager. Sadly, the manager role was the only role into which you could be promoted. Sometimes it worked, and sometimes it didn't. And when it didn't, everybody suffered.

In particular, I remember a woman named Sophia who was good at lending money and wanted to be promoted. She wanted to be the boss because she wanted the recognition that goes with being the boss. She made her wishes known, loudly and clearly. And so, eventually, she got promoted. I'm sure you can predict the outcome. Rather than spending her time coaching her direct reports to help them become better bankers, she—in effect—competed against them, hoping to win their admiration by doing the job better and faster than they could. The result was predictable. Rather than flourishing under her excellent example, her "success" actually had the opposite effect. Her behavior actually *de*-motivated them. And because she devoted her time and energy to *outpacing* them, rather than *developing* them, they seldom improved.

Answer these questions:

→ Are you a collaborator or a lone ranger?

→ Why do you want to be promoted?

→ Are you looking for recognition, or do you really want to lead?

→ Do you want to be the best at what you do, or do you want to lead others who strive to be the best at what they do?

A LEADER LEVERAGES HIMSELF THROUGH OTHERS

Once I'd decided I wanted to become CEO, I could hardly wait to get there. There was so much that I wanted to do, to change, and see happen. This is typical of first-timers. Mostly, I think it's well intentioned, but it's also flawed because it puts too much emphasis on *you*. It shines too much of the spotlight on what *you* can or intend to do, when as a leader, the truth is that you can't actually accomplish that much by yourself.

In some sense, accomplishing things as a leader is about leveraging yourself through others. That's true whether you inhabit the C-suite or lead a division, department, or scout den. In my case, I realized that no CEO of any company of significant size can manage everything alone. In an organization like Silicon Valley Bank, with no tangible assets, the people were the real assets. And people have minds and wills of their own.

If you want to accomplish great things, it's less about you as a leader and what you want and more about how from your leadership position you can construct a culture and a system that allows you to achieve your vision through other motivated people. The catch is, of course, that *their* goals might differ from yours. How can you align your vision with their needs in a way that results in your vision becoming a reality and their needs/desires being met as well? I clearly recall having to face the fact that my title didn't automatically enable me to make my dream a reality. *Having the power or a title and being a true leader are not the same thing.*

Here's an example from corporate life. As it often happens, someone reporting to me asked for a promotion. Not just asked: *begged.* The problem? I couldn't give it because people "promote" themselves. We can't do it for them. A group member who wants to become a leader must start by demonstrating leadership—to the group, not just to the boss. If you promote someone into a leadership position before that person has proven to the group that he or she is ready, the group will reject the promotion. Conversely, if someone proves to the group that he or she can be a leader by inspiring his or her followers to accomplish great things, and if they do so in a way that makes the group want to follow, that person will have prompted his or her own promotion. You'll be forced to promote that person, to legitimize what's already happened without your involvement.

In other words, you can't lead by decree. And you can't make every decision yourself. Position power alone is insufficient. You can give someone a title that implies leadership, but *that person won't succeed as a leader if he or she*:

→ Isn't really a leader (or hasn't yet learned how to lead),

→ Doesn't understand how to communicate their vision to others,

→ Doesn't understand how to enlist other people in the process of realizing their vision,

→ Cannot allow others to feel important and listened to,

→ Cannot delegate execution to others, and—just as important,

→ Cannot allow others to *make decisions regarding execution* without his/her interference.

I recall when our former CEO made me chief banking officer (CBO), a title new to the organization, and moved me from the Massachusetts office I'd helped build to our California headquarters. I'd done pretty well leading in Massachusetts, where we had about thirty-five people by the time I left, but I wasn't ready for a leadership position involving closer to five hundred people. For the first year or two, I achieved very little that wouldn't have been accomplished anyway, and I certainly didn't make much headway on the projects I'd always dreamed of. My title alone was insufficient and probably unnecessary. What I needed, and what I believe I acquired over time, were the skills that would allow me to leverage myself through others, by motivating them to join me in accomplishing my vision. As Antoine de Saint-Exupéry wrote, "One will weave the canvas; another will fell a tree by the light of his ax. Yet another will forge nails, and there will be others who observe the stars to learn how to navigate. And yet all will be as one. Building a boat isn't about weaving canvas, forging nails, or reading the sky. It's about giving a shared taste for the sea . . . "[9]

Almost every organization that you, or I, admire is full of examples of this phenomenon. A leader alone—even a charismatic one—cannot accomplish nearly as much as a confidence-inspiring leadership team that understands how to leverage itself through others, largely by creating and cultivating a culture that reflects its values. This is particularly evident when you contrast competitors you admire with those you don't. An example for me is the difference I observe between Nordstrom and Macy's. I think Nordstrom has done a much better job of weathering the business cycle's ups and downs, largely because its culture inspires employee behavior that keeps customers coming back. I'm sure the people at the top of Macy's would like to succeed, but it's not clear to me that the employees dealing with customers really care that much. I repeatedly hear friends extol the virtues of Nordstrom's sales force, even into the depths of the most recent downturn, comparing them favorably with their Macy's counterparts.

You and your team are capable of more than you know. By setting a good example, describing a vision that inspires others, being authentic and humble yet confident and courageous, learning from your mistakes, and more, you will help your team and organization succeed. "The difference between what we do and what we are capable of doing would suffice to solve most of the world's problems," Gandhi said.[10]

I think that many leaders in today's world put too much emphasis on themselves and not enough on the people who work for and with them. No single leader can accomplish much by himself. To the extent that he tries, he will sub-optimize, if not fail. When President George W. Bush referred to himself as "The Decider," he made himself look silly. When leaders like Steve Jobs (as portrayed

9   Antoine de Saint-Exupéry, "Ouevres," *Citadelle*, (Paris: Gallimard, 1959), Section LXXV (75), 687, accessed April 9, 2018, https://quoteinvestigator.com/category/antoine-de-saint-exupery/.

10   Mohandas Karamchand Gandhi, "Mahatma Gandhi Quotes," BrainyQuote, accessed April 9, 2018, https://www.brainyquote.com/authors/mahatma-gandhi-quotes.

through his biographers), Jack Welch, and so many others, describe their management style in a way that portrays them as the hero, and everyone around them as mindless executors of their will, they unintentionally make themselves look ridiculous.

Great leaders work hard to be good people, set an example for others, build a confidence-inspiring team around them, build a good culture in the organizations they lead, and articulate a vision that inspires others. They make a few big decisions over time about direction, but they leave most decision-making and virtually all execution to their management team and their followers. They are people who inspire others, but they are not superheroes.

Let me end with a negative example. Sometime back, in the course of a reorganization, I promoted someone to head of a division. I'll call her Mary. Prior to this promotion, she'd been one of the best performers in the division, if not the entire bank. But the promotion was not well thought through. Being the best performer at an activity (such as, in our case, lending) does not necessarily imply leadership skills.

Excited about the promotion, Mary was determined to prove herself in this new position. She did what most people do when they've been promoted. She doubled down on the qualities that made her successful in her old job. The problem is the very qualities that made her successful as an individual contributor ultimately made her unsuccessful as a leader. Often, individual contributors make all the decisions by themselves. They don't delegate. They don't have a vision (and don't have to) because what they're responsible for is executing someone else's vision. They don't necessarily have to communicate with others on a regular basis because they often don't have direct reports of their own. In effect, they're running their own "one-man" shop.

Being a leader is totally different. Mary seldom talked with her new direct reports because she wasn't used to sharing and felt it was a waste of time. She had no "vision" for where she wanted to take her division, and she didn't really understand what a vision was.

Accustomed to making all the decisions herself, she didn't see the need to involve others in decision-making. When she did talk with her direct reports, it was to tell them what she'd decided. She rarely asked their opinion.

Over time, her people grew disaffected. One of her "lieutenants" confessed that she felt lonely in her presence. Others said they didn't feel trusted because they weren't allowed to make decisions on their own and weren't invited to participate in her decision-making. Morale sank. Soon, results followed morale.

By not developing and articulating a vision, by not communicating, by not delegating execution and—most important—decision-making around execution, Mary robbed her people of their professional pride, their opportunity to learn and develop themselves through trial and error, and ultimately their joy in their work. As you might expect, the better ones left for greener pastures.

Answer these questions:

→ What does it mean to leverage yourself through others?

→ Do you have the kinds of skills that would enable you to leverage yourself through others?

→ What are those skills?

→ Would you rather read or discuss?

→ Are you interested in other people's opinions, or are you more interested in telling them yours?

→ Would you rather solve a problem by yourself, or coach others to solve it?

PART TWO

THE FUNDAMENTALS OF LEADING

Basic Techniques and Maneuvers

"Do I not destroy my enemies when I make them my friends?"
ABRAHAM LINCOLN

CHAPTER 2

YOU CAN'T DO IT ALONE

Building and Leading a Team

What this chapter is all about:

In this part of the book, we talk about how to choose your team, how to set the tone with your team, and how to cultivate your team over time.

Some of the questions we try to answer are:

→ Should you keep the team you inherit, or should you build a new one?

→ What characteristics should you be looking for in the individual members of your team?

→ Once you've assembled your team, how do you "set the tone"?

→ Teams never stay the same because people are unpredictable. How do you cultivate your team over time?

"We needed the strongest men of the party in the Cabinet.
We needed to hold our own people together.
I had looked the party over and concluded
that these were the very strongest men.
Then I had no right to deprive the country
of their services."[11]

ABRAHAM LINCOLN

CHOOSING YOUR TEAM

Congratulations, you've got the position! You are finally in a leadership role, just like you've always wanted. Either someone chose you, or you've volunteered. Either way, you're signed up. You've spent some time thinking about why you want this new position, and you believe your motivations are good ones. You've taken an honest inventory of your strengths and weaknesses relative to what leadership requires, and you're committed to working on your shortcomings and maintaining your strengths. You're ready to go.

One of your first tasks will be developing your leadership team. More than a single charismatic leader, a successful organization needs good people and a confidence-inspiring management team. With this in mind, the importance of hiring becomes paramount. What kind of people should you hire around yourself? In the end, *you* are responsible for selecting and coaching your team.

Most often, you inherit a team, but under no circumstances should you take your team as a given just because it was there before you. I don't mean that you should simply fire everybody you inherited right off the bat and just start over from square one. But I do mean that *you are responsible for selecting and coaching your team.* Over time, you will want (and need) to assess not only the aptitude, skills, and attitude of each individual team member but also of the team

---

11 Doris Kearns Goodwin, *Team of Rivals: The Political Genius of Abraham Lincoln* (New York: Simon & Schuster Paperbacks, 2005), 319.

as a whole. How well is it constructed? Are the members complementary to each other? Are all "bases" covered, or are there holes
in the team? Do the members work well together? A team is like a
portfolio. Each member has value on a standalone basis. *And,* each
member has value in terms of the extent to which they help to make
the team itself whole. Making sure that the team is whole, and that
each individual member is a good one, is *your* job. This is one of
your first and most important responsibilities.

When I faced this task for the first time, I did what most people
do at the start. Without even realizing it, I gravitated toward hiring
people that I liked. Often, we like people who are nice to us. Often,
being nice to us means noticing our strengths and telling us, even if
only in small and subtle ways, how much they admire us. In short,
they praise us. All of us are greatly tempted to spend time with
people who *compliment* us. But, if we're trying to build an effective
team, we should focus on hiring people who *complement* us, instead.

Maybe you've read the excellent book by Doris Kearns Goodwin,
Team of Rivals: The Political Genius of Abraham Lincoln. If not, you've
probably heard of it. As a confident leader who was authentic and
humble, with a keen interest in other people's strengths and ideas,
Lincoln understood the importance of appointing the best possible team for his Cabinet. After winning the presidential election,
Lincoln gracefully set aside campaign rivalries and chose his former
competitors as Cabinet members. Lincoln had the wisdom, humility, self-awareness, and emotional intelligence to know that he did
not always need to be "right" or have all the answers. He admitted
when he didn't know something and sought counsel from those he
thought would know better. By appointing the most qualified people, he gained an array of complementary skills and diverse experiences to draw upon. By hiring the right people, Lincoln assembled
a Cabinet that was equal to the monumental challenges that the
country would soon face.

"Every member of this administration was better known, better educated, and more experienced in public life than Lincoln,"

wrote Doris Kearns Goodwin. "Their presence in the cabinet might have threatened to eclipse the obscure prairie lawyer from Springfield. It soon became clear, however, that Abraham Lincoln would emerge the undisputed captain of this most unusual cabinet. . . . His success in dealing with the strong egos of the men in his cabinet suggests that in the hands of a truly great politician the qualities we generally associate with decency and morality—kindness, sensitivity, compassion, honesty, and empathy—can also be impressive political resources. . . . When resentment and contention threatened to destroy his administration, he refused to be provoked by petty grievances, to submit to jealousy, or to brood over perceived slights."[12]

Lincoln's strong, complex Cabinet was sometimes very difficult for him to deal with. So how can you incorporate the most helpful aspects of this example while avoiding some of the pitfalls? What kinds of people should you hire? I have six different—yet complementary—answers.

1. Hire for talent, intelligence, and experience

Hire the smartest, most talented, most experienced people you can find. There's no substitute for these characteristics. In this sense, your team should all be the same: smart, talented, and experienced.

2. Hire people who complement (not *compliment*) you

Hire people who complement you and the rest of your team. If you're highly analytical, for example, you need at least some people around you who are more intuitive. If you're a dreamer (in the positive sense), you'll need some executors around you. In other words, your team members should be different in ways that create a vibrant, cohesive whole. Avoid people who frequently tell you how great you are.

---

12 Goodwin, *Team of Rivals,* xvii.

3. Hire for emotional IQ

Hire people with a high degree of "emotional IQ" (shorthand for being capable of working with others on an "adult-to-adult" basis). In my experience, you can plot all people on a spectrum of behavior with "passive-aggressive" people at one end, "obnoxiously assertive" people at the other, and "adult-to-adult" people in the middle. Adult-to-adult people know how to disagree constructively. They speak their minds; they're not passive-aggressive. At the same time, they don't overdo it; they're not obnoxiously assertive. Instead, they're in the middle, disagreeing with each other, as appropriate, on an adult-to-adult level.

Unlike people at extreme ends of the spectrum, adult-to-adult people can settle on a solution and support it thereafter. Passive-aggressive folks go underground and seek to undermine the decision, while obnoxiously assertive ones keep openly fighting it. It's important that all of your team members operate on an adult-to-adult basis with each other and with you.

Is it possible to coach people who are passive-aggressive or obnoxiously assertive, to help them function as adult-to-adult team members? Yes, you can coach them, but it's hard to do—I'll say that. And depending on how ingrained the quality is in a person, you may have some success with it, or you may find that you're fighting a losing battle.

When I became CEO of Silicon Valley Bank, I made the conscious decision to identify all the passive-aggressive people and all the obnoxiously assertive people, and then either to coach them to the middle (adult-to-adult) part of the spectrum, or if that failed, to encourage them to find work elsewhere. It was a multiyear undertaking. Within a couple of years, we'd found all of the obnoxiously assertive people (they are easy to identify because they are so loud and annoying) and either coached them to the middle or invited them to go work elsewhere. The passive-aggressive people, however, are harder to find. Because they always agree with you, you tend to think of them as smart and cooperative, not passive-aggressive.

You don't figure out that they are passive-aggressive until you catch them bad-mouthing you behind your back. That can take years. In any case, the key to success lies in vigilance and patience. Once you figure out which people fit into which category, coach for as long as you can. Only after you've exhausted all remedies, and still have not gotten them to the middle (adult-to-adult) part of the spectrum, should you ask them to leave.

Abraham Lincoln used a high degree of emotional IQ in managing his team, navigating Cabinet rivalries with kindness and sensitivity. "When one of their feelings would be hurt he'd be able to write a letter saying, if I hurt you in any way I did not mean to do so. Forgive me for things that I might do hastily," said Doris Kearns Goodwin. "When he was upset with somebody he would write what he called a hot letter where he would write it all down and then he would put it aside until his emotions cooled down, and then write: Never sent. Never signed. . . . What he essentially did is what a great politician does, which is to understand that human relationships are at the core of political success."[13]

4. Hire for values

It's also important to have a team that shares your values. All of your team members should have the same values. When I use the word "values," here's what I mean: Values are broad statements of belief about proper conduct. For example: "We are principles-based, not rules-based." Or: "We care about all of our constituencies, not just shareholders." Or: "We are determined to be ethical. Ethics are more important than profits." Finding people with similar values (along with all the other characteristics I've described) may be difficult, but it's worth it. *Under any circumstances,* I would keep searching until I found them, or at least found people with values similar

---

13 Doris Kearns Goodwin, interview by Dave Davies, "Doris Kearns Goodwin on Lincoln and His 'Team of Rivals,'" *Fresh Air,* National Public Radio, broadcast November 8, 2005, transcript posted November 15, 2012, accessed April 8, 2018, https://www.npr.org/2012/11/15/165220138/doris-kearns-goodwin-on-lincoln-and-his-team-of-rivals.

enough that they could accept (meaning embrace) the differences, on an adult-to-adult basis, and neither undermine nor openly oppose them.

For example, if one of your cultural beliefs is that it's important to be principles-oriented rather than rules-oriented, it would be a mistake to hire a rules-oriented person. I made this mistake once when I hired someone I'll call Andre to be on my team. Andre and I spent most of our time arguing. He believed a rule was a rule was a rule, without exception. I felt that principle was more important, and if we achieved our goal with a principles-based orientation, it was okay to break a rule.

One of my principles, for example, was never to "cheat" an employee. Management *must* respect employees and support them. One of Andre's rules was that to qualify for a bonus check, a person had to be employed by the company on the day bonus checks were cut. We had a good employee (I'll call him Jan) who wanted to quit in May, take the summer off, and start business school in September. We persuaded Jan to stay for the summer by promising to prorate his bonus through August. Accordingly, Jan quit at the end of August and left for business school. We cut the bonus checks on September 15. Since Jan no longer worked for us, Andre refused to cut him a check. To do so would violate his rule. Not to do so violated my principle. I overrode Andre. We cut a check for Jan.

Ultimately, your team must accept the *values* that you stand for. This is critical. At the top, as a leader, it's *your responsibility* to set the tone for the entire organization. In any leadership position, *you* set the tone for your part of the whole. If you don't, others will—*on their own*. The result: You'll have no cohesive value system. Employees will become confused and demoralized. And you'll never be in a position to move the enterprise toward the realization of the vision you've articulated.

What's a good way to hire people with the same values? One thing I've learned is that it's very hard to find out anything real about people when you're interviewing them because people are generally smart enough to figure out where you're going with a question, what you'd like to hear, and how to deliver an answer that makes you feel good. So a good way to get people to disclose who they are is to pose situations where there would be more than one possible course of action. If I ask you what course of action you'd take in a given situation and why, it gives me a sense of who you are. For example, I'd say something like: "So, you know, here's a situation I'm facing at work right now. We have this problem with an employee—or, we're working on this project—what would *you* do in my shoes?" So, you describe a situation and they have to think about it on the spot. It's not something they can prepare for. If you say to a person, "How hard do you work?" he knows what you want to hear and says, "I work 24/7." Or, if I ask, "What is your biggest weakness?" nine times out of ten I get the same answer: "I'm too conscientious. I work too hard." So, I think it's important to put people in artificial situations that they'll have to think about and say something about. Their answers will be revealing.

5. Hire for core capabilities, not just previous title

When I graduated from business school, I had loads of theoretical knowledge but no firsthand experience. The cases we'd studied really didn't convey the realities of a job, and knowing so little of what the business world was actually like, I had almost no idea what types of jobs were available or what would be right for me. So I "invented" a different way of approaching this problem that helped me find a job. Since then, it's worked for me in helping others do the same.

I start with the person and then work backward into the job. For example, I start by asking what the person's interests and inherent skills are (which in a mature person are largely the same; that is, if we're naturally good at something, we usually like doing it, and vice versa). I believe there are only about fifteen broad categories of basic activities in which a person can engage in life and only about six or seven that are applicable in business. Knowing this makes a job search easier because instead of looking at potentially thousands of job categories and trying to match them up with ourselves, we can start with about nine or ten basic categories. Examples of activities in these categories are:

→ Analyzing (whether it's a poem or a stock, analyzing is analyzing)

→ Problem solving

→ Selling

→ Negotiating

→ Teaching

→ Leading people (as opposed to managing them)

→ Managing people

→ Managing things (or projects) as opposed to people

→ Consulting (providing expertise in a persuasive and helpful manner)

Note: Categories like art and music, athletics, nursing, child (or senior) care, technical fields, engineering, architecture, etc., sometimes do have a place in business settings, but I'm speaking here to the most broadly applicable areas.

Using this approach, I started my own job search by asking myself the following questions:

Which of the following do I enjoy, and which am I good at?

→ Managing people

→ Leading people (different from managing people)

→ Managing tasks (also different from managing people)

→ Analyzing things (in my system, analyzing a poem and analyzing a company's business model are essentially the same and require the same innate skill set)

→ Teaching others about things I've analyzed (again, as we remember from our university days, teachers are not always the best analyzers and vice versa)

→ Selling things

→ Negotiating (different from selling)

→ Consulting

→ Problem solving

Note: Each of these is separate and distinct. Of course, you could be good at more than one. You could even be good at all of them. But, proficiency at one does not necessarily mean proficiency at any of the others. I've met people who are great at, say, "problem solving," but not at any of the others. Sadly, we often promote people into positions of leadership for the wrong reasons. Just because people are good at problem solving doesn't in any way suggest that they would be good at leading. In fact, it could be the other way around. I knew someone who was great at problem solving, and—on the basis of that—was promoted to a position of leadership. Sadly, he spent all of his time solving problems and telling people the answers. Great leaders let problem solvers solve problems, and they focus on leading. Not only did he not do his job, but he denied others (the problem solvers) the opportunity to do theirs.

Once you know what you like and are good at, you can more easily search for an appropriate job. For example, if managing tasks is your thing, seek out positions where that's the main activity.

In the same vein, I would never look for, say, a new marketing manager. Instead, I'd ask myself: In the position I'm envisioning, what activities do I hope this new person will like and be good at? Managing things? Managing people? Persuading others (selling or negotiating)? Leading a team? Analyzing? Teaching? Problem solving? Once I'd answered that question, I would know what to look for.

Accordingly, this approach also helps me when interviewing potential employees. Along with other criteria (values, cultural fit, etc.), it helps guide my line of inquiry.

Months or years after I've hired someone, this approach can help in other ways. If the person "just isn't working out" (either from their point of view or mine), I sometimes ask myself, especially if that person is clearly a cultural fit, if he or she is simply in the wrong position. Perhaps she's managing people but should really be managing things. Perhaps he's analyzing but should be selling. Often we mistakenly place people in positions requiring a completely different skill set than the one they possess and enjoy, and yet—if they're otherwise a good cultural fit—they can be saved to their benefit and that of the organization, with minimal disruption, by just viewing them from this other point of view. Someone might not be a great manager of people, for instance, but that doesn't mean that their contributions in another area aren't just as valuable. It takes all types of skills to build a vibrant, fully functioning team.

Many times we have promoted someone really good into a new position in which they failed miserably because we weren't thinking about *why* we thought they were good in the first place. We just *knew* that they were good. We might have done better if we had stopped for long enough to figure out *why* we were so convinced they were good. If we had thought about the situation in terms of these nine categories instead, we could have avoided a costly failure, for both the individual and the organization. This happens most frequently, in my experience, when we make someone a manager because they are a good salesperson, or when we make someone a leader because they are a good analyzer.

Perhaps the most common mistake in all organizations is to promote someone who is a good manager of people into a position of leadership without trying to figure out if they have the qualities of a good leader. Sometimes it works, and sometimes it doesn't. When it doesn't, it is usually because the person in question lacks vision and the kinds of communication skills that enable them to motivate large groups of people. Good people managers and good leaders are two different things. I am a case in point. I was pretty good at leading, not so good at managing. The former came more or less naturally; the latter was a constant challenge.

When I first started at SVB, HR enlisted a young woman I'll call Rosa to be my assistant. Rosa and I liked each other, but she actually had no relevant skills or aptitude for the job. So she brought me coffee and arranged my office to make it more comfortable. Finally, we discussed the situation. I told her that although the assistant job didn't seem like the right fit for her, she was such a nice person that I wanted her to take the Strong Interest Inventory vocational test to see what type of work might be a better match. The test results indicated that she should be a nurse. Well, Rosa wasn't particularly interested in science, but she went to work in a different capacity at Stanford Hospital. The last time we spoke, she was managing their concierge program. Her job was to walk around the hospital, paying special attention to patients who seemed like good candidates for becoming donors. The caring attitude and empathy that Rosa had displayed as my assistant made her the perfect person to interact with potential donors in the hospital, making sure they felt comfortable and cared for during their stay.

6. Hire for diversity

Your company will be better off if you embrace diversity. Having a diverse group will result in better problem solving and more creativity, as people from different backgrounds will bring a variety of perspectives and approaches to the table.

Diversity is not just defined along racial, ethnic, age, and gender lines; it also means personality and interests, which are doubly important, since the signal to everyone should be that conformity (except to certain specific values) is not just unimportant, it's actively discouraged. The most creative people object most vehemently to conformity. If you encourage (or worse yet, require) conformity, you'll frighten away your most creative workers.

Early in my career, I worked at a bank where everyone knew that proficiency at golf was required for a promotion. Many of the most creative employees were bad golfers. They usually left for greener pastures early in their tenure, resulting in a dearth of creative people in the corporation. The bank was ultimately acquired for the value of its portfolio (not its people).

Some of our very best employees had some of the most unusual hobbies and interests. They—and we—were better for it.

I hope I haven't confused you. If I have, I hope this summary helps:

1. Talent, intelligence, experience—all your team members should be the best you can find.

2. Complementarity—everyone should be different, each representing a different skill set and approach.

3. Emotional IQ—everyone should be the best you can find.

4. Values—everyone should be more or less the same, they should all share your *values.*

5. Core capabilities (rather than title)—everyone should have the core capabilities that are needed in their respective roles.

6. Diversity—here you should be hoping for lots of differences (in terms of beliefs, personal preferences, experiences, hobbies, etc.). Conformity drives out the most creative, talented people. Avoid conformity.

Ask yourself:

→ What are my beliefs about qualities I should look for in assembling my team?

→ Do my recruitment and selection practices reflect those beliefs?

→ To what extent do I consider compatible values in selecting team members?

→ What might I need to rethink and change in forming my team?

→ What am I best at, and what do I enjoy doing? With this in mind, what kind of people do I need to hire around me to complement my natural skill set and create a diverse, vibrant team?

SETTING THE TONE

As a leader, you need to set the tone. That said, certain dynamics may make this difficult unless you're strong, persuasive, and determined.

One of the first obstacles you'll face is that people generally don't like being told what to believe. Two effective approaches will help you here. First, be extra careful to hire people whose values (not their ideas, nor their personalities) are similar to your own.

Remember what we mean by values. "Values" are broad statements of belief around proper conduct. For example: "We are principles-based, not rule-based."

Or: "We care about all of our constituencies, not just shareholders." Or: "We are determined to be ethical. Ethics are more important than profits."

To the extent that you don't share values, you can hear people out and, if you wish, be influenced. Often, if people feel that you've honestly listened to them, they'll go along with you. Just remember, you are the leader, and only you can set the tone.

One of the most annoying mistakes I ever made as CEO falls into the category I'm talking about here. When I was first promoted, our management team was in a state of disrepair. My predecessor and I overlapped, in a sense, for about three years. He'd made it clear to the organization that I was next in line, and he'd "delegated" a lot of the responsibility for running the company to me. At the same time, he wasn't comfortable delegating, and regularly made it clear to me and everybody else that—even though he'd delegated—he really didn't want me to make any big decisions without getting his buy-in first. It was a little like putting me in the driver's seat, but sitting directly behind me in the back seat and—with extra-long arms—steering the car from there. When a management team works like that, people tend to leave. When I finally took over, our management team was in need of repair.

In the first few years, I worked hard to rebuild the management team, but the outcome was less than satisfactory. I made so many hiring errors that the board appeared to be losing confidence. In any case, at one point early on, I recruited three high-level new hires, all with significant experience, in rapid succession. On the surface, each of the three looked good. But all three had come from substantially larger companies, and they each brought with them values more typical of much bigger organizations. One of these values, I learned, was "closed calendars." All three of them believed that the schedules of executives should be treated like "state secrets." Previously, our company had always used "open" calendars; anyone in the organization could see anyone else's calendar online. Having open calendars made it easier to schedule meetings and also took secrecy and therefore suspicion out of the equation. Instead of imagining where people might be, we actually knew.

But these three new executives had all come from larger corporations that practiced "closed" calendars. All three were horrified by our "open" calendar system. They raised such a ruckus complaining about it that, against my better judgment, I relented and gave in to their demand for "closed" calendars. The result was a mini-disaster, to put it mildly. Scheduling became a nightmare. Rumors around who might be where flourished. Within six months, I decided to revert to our old system. There was a sigh of relief throughout the organization. As I learned in time, many perceived the switch from "open" to "closed" as a betrayal of our culture.

As for those three executives, none succeeded at our company. In time, their values proved to be so far removed from ours that working together grew increasingly difficult. Finally, they all quit of their own volition.

Recently, one of my former colleagues at Silicon Valley Bank and I were musing over the fact that I made so many poor hiring decisions in my first few years as CEO. We set our minds to trying to figure out why. In the end, I think that most of my mistakes emanated from two weaknesses. One weakness was that I was in too much of a hurry. Real or imagined, I felt pressure, from the board and from Wall Street. I should have ignored it. Better to delay a hiring decision a little longer than to bring someone on board who won't work out. But, if you do make that mistake, I would strongly recommend correcting that mistake as soon as you realize that you did in fact choose someone who is not going to make it. One of our board members was fond of saying, "The best time to fire someone is the first time that you think of it." That sounds mean-spirited, and yet, in many cases, both parties are better off afterward.

The other weakness was that I put too much emphasis on whether or not I liked the candidate. I'm not suggesting that hiring people you don't like is a good idea. But most good candidates are capable of behaving, at least during the interview process, in a way that will cause you to like them. Much like during a romantic courtship, we not only try to *please the other person*, but we also look for traits in the other person *that please us*. Stick with the list I've provided here, and take your time, and you will do better than I did.

I have observed that there's a part of every person that doesn't want a boss. Part of every person instinctively wants to rebel against any authority figure, and bosses are authority figures. My predecessor once warned me that the minute I became CEO, I'd have a bull's-eye on my back. The remedy? First, be very careful to hire people with values similar to your own. Second, encourage them to tell you when they disagree with you. Be accessible and open-minded. Hear them out. And then, talk with them about the differences, less in terms of the situation at hand, and more in terms of differences in your underlying values. Don't leave these differences unaddressed. Try to reconcile them.

If you are closed-minded and unwilling to listen to opinions other than your own, you may think your team members agree with your values when they really do not. Often they'll disguise their view as someone else's, like: "Personally, I agree with you, but a lot of other people think the opposite."

My predecessor was quite judgmental. People who disagreed were afraid to say so. We had a great head of HR whom we often appointed to represent us vis-à-vis the CEO, especially when our group disagreed with him. Unfortunately, our head of HR was just as scared of the boss as we were. So, as ridiculous as this oddly useful technique will sound, sometimes he used a puppet to get his (our) point across. Since we were afraid to tell the CEO when we thought he was wrong, our head of HR would don a sock puppet and—pretending to be a ventriloquist—tell the CEO what we really thought, with all of us sitting nervously by, waiting to see his response. Truth be told, this whole thing was borderline ridiculous. Can you imagine sitting in a conference room with eight or ten grown-ups and watching while one of them talks through a goofy-looking sock puppet to another adult who is—not coincidentally—the boss? On one hand, it *was* ridiculous. On the other hand, it worked, in that it introduced an element of humor and depersonalized the experience. The CEO couldn't get as mad at us as he might have otherwise because it was just a sock puppet expressing the objection. Ideally, you will be the kind of leader who others feel comfortable coming to and expressing their views—without a sock puppet!

More than once I've had employees voice agreement, but quickly add that others disagreed. I've learned over time that in most cases, they were trying to protect themselves by projecting their own disagreement onto others. The solution? If we're talking about values, be especially conscientious about hiring people with similar values. If people have already been hired and have different values, they will have to agree to go along with your values. If we're talking about emotional IQ, be particularly careful to hire people who operate in the middle of the spectrum, on an adult-to-adult basis. As regards yourself, try to be as approachable as possible. Remember, you may view yourself as eminently approachable, but your title renders you less so. And if you lack self-awareness, your behavior may also render you less approachable.

Finally, encourage others to state their opinions. And don't immediately disagree when they do. Take time to consider the merit in the opinions being offered up, and to praise their positive aspects. *To see the merit in another person's opinion does not bind you to accept it as your own.* But it may help you make a better decision. In the end, though, you're the leader, and it's your right to make the final decision. In fact, it's your *obligation*.

You can't expect people to be happy all the time, especially when you've made a decision they don't agree with. Since you have the final word, just know that some people will be unhappy sometimes.

There may also be times when you have had the final word and then turned out to be wrong. Admitting that you made a mistake is good. Wishing you'd acquiesced to those who disagreed is not. Necessarily. Consider General Robert E. Lee and his most accomplished general, James Longstreet, at the Battle of Gettysburg. Longstreet saw that the long-range repeater rifle had forever changed warfare, so an offensive battle no longer made sense, particularly if the enemy occupied high ground, as the Union Army did at Gettysburg. Not recognizing this, Lee planned to scale the heights and attack the Union Army. Longstreet disagreed, recommending that the Southern Army abandon Gettysburg, occupy high ground closer to Washington, DC, and get the Union Army to attack him there. Lee listened to Longstreet, as he should have, and decided, as was his responsibility. Wrongly, he attacked at Gettysburg. Lee's mistake cost the Southern Army the Battle of Gettysburg, and ultimately the war. Afterward, Lee admitted his error, as he should have, but did not regret making the decision. As commander-in-chief, it was his duty to decide, even if wrong, as long as he acted in good conscience. Doing otherwise would have undermined the authority of his and everyone else's command down through the ranks, inviting chaos into the Southern Army.[14]

Even the best leaders make mistakes. What separates the good from the great is the willingness to make the hard decisions—even if wrong in retrospect—admit to them, live with the consequences, and learn from them.

In 1862, Abraham Lincoln told his Cabinet that he'd decided to issue an Emancipation Proclamation to free the slaves. He would listen to the Cabinet members' comments as he had all along, he told them, but his decision was already made. Lincoln could not fully know the effects of the Emancipation Proclamation, but knowing that it was the *moral* decision, he also knew it was the right one. "As I would not be a slave, so I would not be a master," Lincoln said. "This expresses my idea of democracy. Whatever differs from this, to the extent of the difference, is no democracy."[15]

In summary, *values* are the *bedrock* of culture. It is of the utmost importance that your team shares common values. To the extent that they don't, *you* have to set the tone. To accomplish this, it is important that you encourage an open atmosphere where people are free to discuss differences. For this to happen, your direct reports

---

14 *Michael Shaara, The Killer Angels* (New York: Random House, 2003).

15 Abraham Lincoln, "August 1, 1858: Definition of Democracy," in *Lincoln on Slavery,* National Park Service: Lincoln Home, National Historic Site, accessed April 8, 2018, https://www.nps.gov/liho/learn/historyculture/slavery.htm.

must perceive you as open-minded and nonjudgmental. Only you can ensure that they do; i.e., you actually have to be open-minded and nonjudgmental.

If a disagreement arises (as, for example, with the open-calendars versus closed-calendars), these disagreements need to be discussed. As it turns out, most disagreements don't actually involve differences in values, they are simply differences of opinion. But some do, like in the case I described. And when they do, they need to be resolved. You don't always have to have your way, except to the extent that the disagreements emanate from real differences in important values. And in the case I described, they did. You need to identify the underlying value and persuade the people who disagree. In the end, to the extent that important differences in values cannot be resolved, somebody will have to go.

A WORD ON TURNOVER

Turnover is inevitable for two reasons. First, there are changing situations. People get married, they have children, they get depressed, they get sick, they have to move, someone recruits them away, they lose interest and burn out, etc. Second, the team evolves, and—with it—their role in the team evolves. Sometimes, they evolve with it; sometimes they do not. You, as the leader, have to be ever mindful of not only the "health" of each individual team member but of the "health" of the team as a whole. The result: Turnover is inevitable. Sometimes it is voluntary, sometimes you will have to initiate it.

When I was CEO at SVB, we regularly weeded out team members who were not working out. This is a positive organizational move, but only if handled correctly. There's a world of difference between telling people directly that you're upset with their behavior (but giving them an honest chance to shape up) and bullying or browbeating them in your frustration. More than once, we had interventions. That setting has the advantage of complete honesty.

The problem is laid out on the table, and everyone concerned can determine the appropriate next step. Bullying, by contrast, is completely counterproductive. Beyond all else, it's unethical, even if it ends up helping the bottom line.

One of my first bosses, at the beginning of my career, had a different approach. Let's call him Rick. Rick felt that coaching was difficult and burdensome, and that firing was dangerous. Instead, he just "bullied" people out of the organization. If he wanted someone to go, he abused them (where possible in public) until they decided to leave of their own volition. Needless to say, I cannot recommend this approach.

From time to time, coaching—and even interventions—don't lead to the result you're looking for. Sometimes you have to fire someone. If you're at all compassionate, you'll find this difficult. If you don't find it difficult, you should *not* be in a position of leadership.

If you do have to fire people, here are the most important things to remember:

First, although it doesn't feel like it, at a certain level you're doing them a favor. They're doubtless as unhappy with you as you are with them. They're likely competent, but just not a good fit, either in the sense that they're in the wrong job (relative to their innate skill set), or in the sense that they're in the wrong company (relative to their values). You're not condemning them as human beings. Instead, you're recognizing that the fit is not a good one. They need to separate in order to find an environment and a boss that represent a good match. Once they have found these, they will be happier. You are releasing them in order to give them a better chance to be happy.

Second, your job is to release people, not to degrade them. Do not fall victim to the temptation to read them a laundry list of their shortcomings. It may make you feel better in that it may allow you to feel more justified in firing them. However, it will not make them feel any better, and it will open you up to gratuitous disagreement.

Disagreement will lead to fruitless, frustrating altercation. And the end will be the same: separation. Only this time with the addition of bitterness. Stick with your original reason and do not deviate from it: the fit is not a good one.

Allow people to leave with dignity. They will be happier, you will be happier, and their former colleagues will be happier. But don't expect those who remain to express appreciation. As much as their former colleagues may have wished for them to be fired, they will neither admire you nor love you for being the one who carried it out.

Ask yourself:

→ What do I do now to set the tone for my team, unit, or organization?

→ What might I do differently to set a better tone?

→ How do I plan to deal with resistance, disagreement, reluctance to speak, or other obstacles I encounter in setting a different tone?

→ What will I do when I make a decision that turns out to be wrong?

→ Am I genuinely approachable?

→ Do I encourage others to state their opinions and take time to consider the merit in the opinions being offered up?

→ What do I do when I discover that I have hired or inherited someone who belongs in another organization, but not mine?

→ What do my answers to the questions above say about the value I place on setting the tone for my organization?

CHAPTER 3

BUILDING A GREAT CULTURE

Care About Me, Help Me Grow,
Describe to Me the Promised Land,
and Lead Me to It

THE IMPORTANCE OF CULTURE

You are the leader. Your two most important tasks are building the leadership team and building the culture. Chapter 2 explored the initial phase of building the leadership team—namely, hiring and setting the tone. This chapter talks about building the culture. It will help you find answers to the questions: *How do I want the people in my organization to treat each other? What will be the "rules of engagement"?*

When I was in business school thirty-eight years ago, the culmination of our two-year program was "strategy." The business school I went to prided itself on molding future leaders, and the curriculum made it clear that the study of business culminates in "strategy": the jewel in the crown.

My experience in these past thirty-eight years has given me a different opinion. In my view, culture almost always trumps strategy. Strategy is your longer-term game plan. It speaks to the mind. Culture is the sense of knowing what it means to live/work in your company/organization/tribe/group. It speaks to the heart. In my experience, the heart drives the mind more than the other way around. Additionally, if you have a good strategy but a bad culture, you will lose over time. If you have a good culture but a bad strategy, however, you will regroup and develop a better strategy.

Culture motivates us. It enables us to know what to do. It guides us in our hiring, managing, evaluating, and rewarding. Culture gives our lives meaning. If we have a good culture, we know why we get up in the morning. In my view, the best leaders focus on building the leadership team and building the culture first, and then they turn to formulating the strategy. And, finally, culture guides us in the way we treat others. Culture is all about how we treat each other, how we work together.

WHAT IT MEANS TO WORK HERE

When I joined Silicon Valley Bank in 1990, it was immediately clear that everyone who worked there *knew what it meant to be an SVB'er.* First, we all had an attitude, and if we didn't arrive with it, we soon acquired it. The attitude was, *we're winning!!!* Second, there was a body of rules, some of which seemed silly at first, that we *all* followed with immense pride. Third, we *all* knew our mission: *to help entrepreneurs succeed.* No one had any doubt about these things. When we interviewed candidates for positions at SVB, we could immediately tell whether they were right for us. When evaluating employees, we knew whether they were doing the right things. When rewarding employees, we knew what they deserved. Even better, all SVB'ers knew what it meant to work at SVB and whether they belonged. Those who stayed were proud and excited about being there.

Everything that happens in an organization is a result of its culture. A corporation's culture emanates from the CEO through top leadership to the rest of the corporation. This type of structure also applies to other kinds of organizations. Before you can consciously build a culture, you must know who you are, what your values are, and what values you'd like your team to emulate. If any discrepancy exists between these two sets of values, you must identify that discrepancy and do everything possible to change your behavior so it reflects your targeted values.

Your culture is of the utmost importance. It is your *culture* that enables you to attract and retain the talent you want, and avoid the talent you don't want. Ultimately, there's no such thing as a good or bad employee—only those who fit into your culture and those who don't. You'll get and keep what you deserve, so make sure that what you deserve is what you want. Remember, left to itself, everything seeks alignment. Your team members will copy you, they'll hire and retain others who fit the same mold, and they'll reject any errors they make in hiring. Even if they don't, those errors will reject themselves. *Be who you want your team members to be, and the rest will take care of itself.*

I've read many studies over the years about why some people stay with companies and others move on. There are many factors to consider: Do people think they're paid enough? Do they like the work? Do they like their co-workers? Do they like their boss? Whether they think they're being paid enough is a question of whether you're paying "at market." Pay at market, and—all other factors being equal—you'll only lose employees to companies that overpay. Whether people like their work depends on whether you have them in the right job. Whether they like their co-workers and boss is ultimately a question of culture. People like working with others who share their values, and they like reporting to people with similar values *and* good leadership skills. I'll discuss leadership training later, but for now, people are happiest when they feel they belong. A place where they belong is one that reflects values similar to their own.

Building a culture is in large measure creating a set of norms that people conform to. *The main thing is that people know what it means to be a member of your team.*

Alexander the Great, for example, earned his army's loyalty through actions that created a unifying culture for his troops, which encompassed different cultures and languages. Alexander fought alongside his men in battle, leading the charge into the heart of danger. He also personally sacrificed for them. One instance occurred when Alexander's army was desperate for water after weeks of marching through a desert. Thousands of his men had already died of thirst, illness, and heatstroke on that march, and the rest feared they would not make it out of the Gedrosian desert alive. As Philip Freeman writes:

> *Toward the end of the march . . . some scouts found a small spring with only enough water to fill a single helmet. The patrol was so thankful that they had found even this that they brought it before Alexander, who was as thirsty as anyone. As wretched as his own state was, however, he knew his men were suffering even more. Therefore, just as he had done in the desert crossing in Bactria four years earlier, Alexander refused to drink when his army could not. He took the helmet of precious water and poured it on the ground in full view of his army. To the parched men, for their king to share in their suffering in this way meant more than the water soaking into the sand. They were so heartened, says Arrian, it was as if they had each drunk every drop that he poured on the ground.*[16]

Alexander the Great inspired his men and earned their trust time and again. He treated his troops with respect, and they returned that respect, following him undefeated into battle after battle.

Through many means, large and small, we create culture in daily life. When I started at SVB, I discovered a clearly defined set of norms that almost seemed designed to annoy me. But everyone at

---

16 Philip Freeman, *Alexander the Great* (New York: Simon & Schuster Paperbacks, 2011), 29.

SVB practiced them, and people were proud to do so. Whenever you join a group, some of the requirements may, frankly, seem stupid. A new member's understandable reaction is to feel put off. Over time, though, people come to feel pride in these practices because they're an integral part of being a member of that community.

For example, SVB's first CEO, Roger Smith, was the perfect person for building a unique culture. He was a man of strongly held opinions. He thought, for instance, that we should never lend people money until they had deposited at our bank for a while first. Prior to SVB, I'd worked at a bank where it was the other way around (loan first, deposit second). Roger wanted everyone in the bank to carry deposit account opening forms in the trunk of their car. Deposits are the lifeblood of a bank, after all. Without deposits, a bank could not make loans. If Roger went on a call with you, he'd do a "trunk check." That's right, he would actually say, "Open your trunk," and would check to see if you had the forms inside. It may sound odd, but coming to SVB was at first very difficult.

Frankly, the SVB approach felt kind of paternalistic and even insulting to me at times. But I've come to realize that we all have the power to perceive situations like that as either insulting or humorous. If you want to be successful in life, you've got to see things you find odd as being humorous in one way or another, rather than insulting. It relaxes you and opens your mind to new experiences. You can choose to make life into a game so it ends up being fun, or you can be deadly serious about it and be stressed all the time. Similar situations I ran into at SVB were that we each had to have a small, "secretary-size" blue-covered book with us at all times and keep a running diary of everything that happened during the day. If Roger caught you without your "bluebook," you were in for an immediate reprimand. It felt so stupid at first. But, people grew proud of the number of bluebooks they'd filled in their years at the bank. In the end, however, the regulators put a stop to it; they wanted us to prepare a separate file for each individual company, rather than chronologies of the life of a lender. The bluebook method made it difficult to find things, and ultimately the regulators objected. Another example: Roger took roll each morning, and if he wanted to check up on you, at 5:00 p.m. as well. Individually, we all hated this norm. But oddly enough, even people like me began to feel some pride in it. Whether you were in trouble or doing okay, you knew where you stood.

Think critically about these types of things and make an effort to inculcate values into your organization and to create a culture that helps to point all of your team members in the right direction, feel that they belong, and know where they stand. By doing so, you can create an atmosphere of trust and loyalty among your team members.

THE VALUE OF VALUES

I'd like to take a moment to discuss SVB's values. I don't mean to imply that every organization needs to adopt this particular set to succeed. But for us, they were the right ones—the backbone of our alignment and a reflection of what I, and those who worked closely with me, believed in. These values helped us attract and retain excellent employees over the years and gave our existing employees a sense of being in a place where they belonged.

Our values evolved over time. I was the third CEO, leading SVB's third management team, and each team had its own set of values. Of course, after the first CEO, each subsequent leader took the helm of the ship with a preexisting set of values and had to subtract, retain, and add in order to arrive at a set of their own. Only our first CEO had the benefit of starting with a blank slate. Rather than reviewing my predecessors' complete sets, I'll describe the values we retained from each respective era.

From our first CEO's era, we continued to value "winning" in the market. When SVB began, we were a David among a handful of Goliaths. Winning was survival, survival was everything, and so winning was everything. Greeting employees in the hallway, our first CEO used to stop us midstride, look us straight in the eye, give a thumbs-up, and say, "Hey, we're winning!" Literally. Unlikely as this may seem, it happened daily. He even issued each of us an official company tote bag with the inscription, "We're winning!" The desire to win and the enjoyment and celebration of our wins remained important parts of SVB's culture.

Even in those early days, we "won" on a regular basis. Part of our success, at least in the eyes of Wall Street, was because we were extremely cost-effective. For almost ten years running, we had one of the best (meaning lowest) efficiency ratios in the United States—quite a feat, since there were over ten thousand banks in the United States at the time. "Efficiency ratio" refers to the amount of money required to bring in a dollar of revenue (obviously, the lower the better). But there was a price to be paid in going too low. We kept our efficiency rating low by not building infrastructure. We had no internal audit function, no HR department, and very little in the way of systems. Ultimately, this all caught up with us.

Our second CEO—brought in to remedy the fact that we had too few processes or systems to support our growth—had to double our headcount in a single year in order to build the missing infrastructure. That's a lot of people to quickly assimilate into an existing culture. Each new employee came from a different company (i.e., a different culture), and because they all viewed themselves as having been brought in to fix something broken, they all felt they'd come from better places. Most weren't shy about showing it. The result was a sort of Tower of Babel. We went through a period where, on average, people weren't treating each other very well. The new employees treated the old ones like a vanquished people, and they treated each other like folks who just didn't know what was best for the organization.

So our second CEO did something brilliant; later I learned that he'd done this successfully at every company he'd led. He identified the top fifty employees in our hierarchy, put them in a room together, and divided them into teams of four or five. He gave each team a table, and on each table placed a set of about one hundred fifty small pieces of paper, on each of which was printed a noun describing a virtue: "trust," "dependability," "sincerity," etc. He then asked us to group the papers into piles of concepts that were similar. Each table ended up with ten or twelve piles. Then he asked us to pick the five or six piles containing the concepts that we'd most like to define our culture, and in each case to identify a single word that exemplified the pile. Using a moderator, he asked the groups to all work together to build a list of eight values we could agree on. Amazingly, this group of fifty warring parties had no trouble—in eight hours or so—coming up with a set of eight values that we could all be enthusiastic about. If we'd taken the next step and tried to summarize the eight into a single phrase, it would have read something like, "Work hard, take responsibility, and treat each other well."

Now, it took us several years after this exercise to iron things out. By that, I mean it took about that long for the people whose behavior didn't really reflect these eight values to leave, and—just as important—to leave before they'd managed to hire more people whose behavior didn't match our values and who would, for the same reason, ultimately leave.

Values are not just the glue that holds an organization together and gives it a unique sense of identity. Values also allow an organization to become more or less self-governing. They are the "voice of the conscience" that enables your employees to know what to do, even when you or another member of your leadership team is not there to tell them.

Fear or "Love"?

According to Richard Nixon, "People react to fear, not love. They don't teach that in Sunday school, but it's true."[17] In my experience, nothing could be further from the truth. When people operate in an atmosphere of fear, they become less creative and more

17 Richard Nixon, "Richard Nixon Quotes," BrainyQuote, accessed June 3, 2021, https://www.brainyquote.com/quotes.richard_m_nixon_400958.

protective, less open and more "political." First of all, I think that President Nixon was using a false dichotomy. I would substitute the word "encouragement" for the word "love." That said, my experience tells me that our best employees respond much more productively to encouragement than to fear. Fear may work better than encouragement with some people. I'm not sure those people are the ones you want in your organization.

SCHOOLS OF GOVERNANCE:
Cops and Robbers vs. the Voice of the Conscience

Under my leadership as the third CEO, I believe we added considerably to our corpus of values. My predecessors subscribed to a view of banking and human nature totally different from my own. In commercial banking, there are two schools of governance: 1) "cops and robbers," and 2) "voice of the conscience."

Adherents of the "cops and robbers" school believe that the world consists of two types of people: salespeople and responsible people. The salespeople, or lenders, are the "robbers." They'll do anything to make a sale, regardless of its impact on the bank's bottom line or the shareholders' well-being. As a result, you also need responsible people in banking, namely the "cops," to counterbalance the lenders. They are the staff, the credit people, and the regulators who keep the salespeople in check and prevent them from doing any harm. I understand why this is the prevalent school of thought in the commercial banking sector, but I think it is counterproductive in two ways. First, it pits people against each other in a way that causes rifts that never heal. Second, because the two sides are driven by two different sets of competing rules, in the absence of a clear hierarchy, or a Solomon, outcomes end up being the result of whoever has the more persuasive verbal skills, or the more forceful personality, or just more "political clout." In other words, it creates a kind of "might makes right" atmosphere. Whether a prospective loan is a good one often gets lost in the struggle.

Adherents of the "voice of the conscience" school believe that the organization's norms must be ingrained in everyone, regardless of role. Lenders (salespeople) must be as aware of and concerned about the credit side as they are about the sales side. In short, they need to be "whole" people, as do all staff members, including the credit people. (For a bank to function really well, lenders must be as aware of the credit side as the sales side; correspondingly, credit people must be as concerned about the sales side as the credit side.)

These two schools of thought are best illustrated by some experiences from my first few years in banking.

I started my banking career at the Shawmut Bank in Boston, a venerable old organization now owned by Bank of America. Our chief credit officer was in his sixties when I joined Shawmut, and he'd been there all his professional life. Like Shawmut as a whole, he subscribed to the "voice of the conscience" school of banking. A natural teacher, he couldn't resist a speech whenever he found himself in front of a group of lenders. His speeches often included something like this: "If you find yourself in disagreement with the Credit Committee even once, you should go home, look in the mirror, and ask yourself, 'Why?' If you find yourself in disagreement with the Credit Committee off and on again after that, you should go home and ask yourself, 'Do I belong at Shawmut?' And if you find yourself in regular disagreement with the Credit Committee, you should be asking, 'Do I really belong in lending?'" He wanted to impress on the salespeople that it wasn't "us versus them" or "line versus staff," but rather that it was important to care about the entire organization. In short, he wanted each of us lenders to be self-governing.

In my third year at Shawmut, a large money-center bank closed its loan production office in Boston's financial district, and the various Boston banks scooped up all their lenders. We, in Shawmut's technology lending group, hired Tom, a "born sales guy," if there really is such a thing. He'd grown up in a "cops and robbers" culture, as was prevalent in all the money-center banks then (and is now, I suspect).

Tom did what sales guys do: He brought in business. But as time went by, we saw that his choices were somewhat indiscriminate. His biggest win in his first couple of years was taking one of the large (and failing) mini-computer companies away from our closest competitor, the Bank of New England. By that time, mini-computer companies (DEC, Wang, Data General, Prime) were already in decline as the personal computer and so-called workstations (SUN, Apollo, etc.) had begun their ascent.

I'd also learned through the market grapevine that Tom's "win" wasn't as glorious as he'd led us to believe, since the Bank of New England had already asked that company to leave the bank due to poor performance. The Wall Street analysts found few kind things to say about that mini-computer company at the time. So one night after work, while chatting with Tom, I asked, "Why did you fight so hard to bring this company into the bank knowing it's in a state of decline and that most people believe it will never recover?"

"Hey," said Tom, in his raspy, devil-may-care voice, "I just bring them in and throw them up against the wall, and if they stick, hey, it's the credit people's problem, not mine."

Tom cared very little for anyone's well-being but his own. That's not an attitude I'd want in a prospective team member.

THINKING HORIZONTALLY

I was not about to continue with the "cops and robbers" culture established by my predecessors now that I was CEO and responsible for setting the tone. To me, this smacked of "parent and child" culture. I wanted adults populating my bank. I think there's no room for either "parents" or "children" in business. I didn't want our "staff" people treating our "line" people (in fact, I never use the terms "staff" and "line") like children, nor did I want the "line" people treating the "staff" people like parents. And I didn't want *anyone* in the bank treating our clients, particularly those who had fallen on hard times, like "children," as many banks do. Commercial banks are notorious for acting *in loco parentis* to borrowers whose businesses are suffering.

No, I wanted adults who would treat those around them (both inside and outside the bank) like adults and expect them to behave the same way. This meant no "children," no "parents," no passive-aggressive people, and no obnoxiously assertive people. If you hire people who are all intelligent, who come from diverse backgrounds and so bring a wide variety of experiences, and *who know how to work collaboratively on an adult-to-adult basis,* you can't help but succeed.

Collaborating means two things: 1) knowing how to work together on an adult-to-adult basis with members of your own team, and 2) knowing how to work together successfully with other teams and business units. Many organizations, and many managers within organizations, don't know how to work together collaboratively with other teams. Consider the words of one of my first bosses at Shawmut: "Life in corporations is a struggle for scarce resources. Never, ever give in to anyone from any other group in the bank."

Deliberately or inadvertently, most organizations encourage competition between functional areas and even between groups within functional areas. Most managers do the same. Too many managers view themselves as the aristocracy and their departments as their fiefdoms. For most managers in most corporations, for example, the first questions are: "What's in it for us? What's best for our group?" At SVB, our first questions were: "What's best for the bank as a whole? What's best for the customers? What's best for the employees? What's best for the shareholders?"

Many people in business believe it's important to have internal groups competing against each other. I think that's a terrible idea. These types of leaders often create an incentive structure that encourages competitive behavior between individuals and between groups. If you don't change the incentive structure, most people will do what the money dictates, whether their behavior benefits anybody other than themselves, or not.

Many managers, particularly those who see things in black and white, struggle with the concept of doing what's best for the organization rather than what's best for their individual unit. When you ask them to take a global, enterprise-wide view rather than a limited, parochial view—often described as "horizontal" versus "vertical" thinking—they feel you're denying the validity of the "truth" that they and their group are there to defend. Nothing could be further from the *actual* truth.

It can be difficult for team members to understand the importance of thinking horizontally instead of vertically. At the simplest level, almost every group would like a disproportionate portion of the corporation's bonus pool to split among its members. At a slightly higher level, each department tends to feel it's the most important. Finance would love it if nobody ever spent any money so they could use what's not spent (minus the amount they think they need for computer systems to support their work and perhaps for a few additional headcount) to make the bottom line bigger. HR would be delighted if they could get everyone in the organization to enroll in (and actually attend) a bunch of training programs so they could justify a larger learning and development staff. Compliance would be ecstatic if they could get each employee to take all thirty-odd compliance-training modules annually to help prove to regulators that the company is on top of compliance requirements. In many banks, the lenders would be thrilled to eliminate the need for credit analysis, paperwork, pricing hurdles, and consistency so they could please every client, every time. The list goes on.

Here's the thing: If we don't satisfy our customers' needs, they'll leave us. No single division or function can by itself satisfy the customers' needs. Not finance. Not HR. Not compliance. Not operations. Not sales. None. If they don't work together to satisfy the customers' needs, it just won't happen. When divisions work together, no single function should dominate. Not finance. Not HR. Not even sales. The overriding goal has to be to satisfy the customer, not to satisfy the dictates of the head of finance, HR, sales, etc. Functional teams (like the "finance team," "HR team," or "sales team") are of little value; only "cross-functional teams" can satisfy the customers' needs in a way that allows the entire company to survive and flourish.

What we achieved at SVB, and what still makes me proud, is that we built a culture in which almost everyone could see the big picture and the need for balance within it. That kind of culture is essential to optimizing any large organization. I believe it's a rarity in corporate America, but it is achievable.

We did this largely through implementing the concept of cross-functional teams. This means that teams would come together, often spontaneously, to help a client. Such teams would include members of all of the various disciplines: lending, credit, operations, compliance, etc. Each team member had the obligation to apprise the team of the viewpoint of his/her individual discipline, but not to insist on it. Rather, the ultimate solution, designed to satisfy the customer, had to be fashioned in a way that met the basic requirement of each individual discipline, but in a way *that kept the client as happy as possible.* In other words, the ultimate solution always ended up in a series of compromises. But, in doing it this way, we learned to do what was best for the bank, even if it wasn't always ideal from an individual department's point of view.

We encouraged our managers to make decisions based on what was best for the *whole* corporation and accordingly the shareholders—not what was best for the managers or their individual functional area. In short, we charged each manager with the responsibility of making decisions *as if he or she were CEO.* I call this being horizontal rather than vertical.

We rewarded this kind of behavior. When it came time to decide on bonuses, cross-functional teams of managers decided on them. For example, a finance employee's bonus was determined not just by the head of finance, but rather by a cross-functional team of managers based on whether the recipient worked effectively with members of the other disciplines. We required *everyone* to make decisions as if he or she were CEO for the benefit of *all* of our constituencies.

A bad example: Once, in the very early years at SVB, we had a CFO who, although brilliant, was decidedly *not* horizontal in his orientation. One day, he decided to revise the policy governing reimbursement of expenses for those who had to travel for work. First and foremost, this policy applied to salespeople. He had spent his whole life in California and worked at our "headquarters" in Santa Clara at the time. I don't believe he had ever been to New England where my office was located. Nor had he ever been in sales. As a result, he didn't realize that in New England it was easy to visit two, three, or even four states in a single day. And he didn't realize that a salesperson who relied on public transportation could waste whole days trying to visit a single customer or prospect. And so, one of the rules in his new policy was: "Employees had to take public transportation." Another was: "Employees could not cross state lines without the written permission of a member of the Managing Committee." It was laughable. I imagined myself in a bus, on the Massachusetts/Rhode Island line, asking the bus driver to stop for a minute so I could go to a store with a fax machine and request written permission from a senior executive at SVB to cross the border. His goal: *save money.* But he was oblivious to the real questions: What's best for the bank? For the customer? For the employees? And, finally, for the shareholders?

THE ROLE OF RESPONSIBILITY

"As I've said before,
this is not the life I chose; it chose me.
But I accepted the responsibility
and I've never wavered in my commitment."[18]

BENAZIR BHUTTO

At SVB, we emphasized responsibility. That said, its effect on the culture hinges on how one defines responsibility.

There are various levels of responsibility. At the lowest level, the individual says, "I'll admit, I did it and I did it wrong. I wish I'd done it differently. I'll take the blame." Ultimately, this type of admission has little positive benefit for the organization, except perhaps to end finger pointing. At the highest level (the level we target), the individual says: "I'll admit, I did it and I did it wrong. I wish I'd done it differently. I'll take the blame and *I will take responsibility for fixing it!"*

THE SPECTRUM OF HUMAN BEHAVIOR

Have you ever noticed in meetings that some people don't say anything and others say a lot? Some people appear to hold back to see what the boss or at least the most outspoken members of the team think, and then they chime in, in apparent agreement. On the other side of the coin, some people love to argue, and others even seem to derive joy from crushing other people's points of view with "superior" arguments of their own. Some people are almost obsequious, while others are clearly combative. Imagine a spectrum, with obsequious people at one end and combative people at the other:

---

18 Benazir Bhutto, interview and article by Ginny Dougary, "Destiny's Daughter," *HuffPost*, accessed April 9, 2018, https://www.huffingtonpost.com/ginny-dougary/destinys-daughter_b_434530.html.

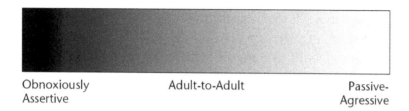

Obnoxiously   Adult-to-Adult   Passive-
Assertive   Agressive

If we arbitrarily place combative people at the left end of the spectrum and obsequious people at the right end, then we can call those in the middle the "adult-to-adult" people. I call the people at the left end "obnoxiously assertive" and the people at the right end "passive-aggressive."

The obnoxiously assertive people bully their way to victory. The passive-aggressive people allow themselves to be dominated by the people on the left. In meetings, they'll nod and agree, and then later in the hallway, will whisper about what jerks those obnoxiously assertive people are. In my view, only the adult-to-adult people are earning the money we pay them. The adult-to-adult people express themselves in meetings, sharing with the group their opinions, experience, and wisdom. They do so in a mature way, neither dominating nor deferring.

When I became CEO in 2001, I made it a priority to transform all the obnoxiously assertive people as well as the passive-aggressive people into adults. We would either coach them to the middle, or if they could not be coached, we would ask them to leave. It took a few years, but we accomplished much of the transformation we were targeting. Within a couple of years, all of the obnoxiously assertive people were gone. But there are still, I believe, a few passive-aggressive people out there. The bullies are easier to find than the wimps. When someone yells, we know they're bullying. But when someone just nods in agreement, we can't immediately tell if they're adults who genuinely agree or wimps just pretending to agree. Finding all of the passive-aggressive people can sometimes take years.

We'll return to this spectrum later to help us understand the nuances of decision-making in a group setting.

DOGSLEDS VS. ORCHESTRAS

A few years ago, I met a man from Denmark who was serving in a special unit of the country's military. He was a member of a small group of soldiers who patrol Greenland, and by doing so, maintain Denmark's claim to this large body of largely uninhabited land. Most of the year, they traveled in subzero weather from one place to another over ice and snow using dogsleds. What I found most interesting was that at night they had to tether the dogs at safe distances from each other because if they didn't, the dogs would kill each other.

From a distance, these dogs all seem happily engaged in a group effort, and to a certain extent, that's true. But that's only on the surface. Underneath, a strict hierarchy exists among them. Each knows where he stands relative to the others. Each occupies his unique place in the hierarchy. Most interesting: Each would like most to advance, to replace the dog ahead of him. So, each is constantly looking for indications of weakness in the dog in front of him, and if he senses it, he may well attack with the intent to kill.

Many groups operate like these dogs. And many leaders endorse this model, thinking that it brings out the best in each participant. To me, the disadvantages inherent in this model are obvious. Besides creating an unpleasant atmosphere, this model engenders a constant, nagging—and in many cases debilitating—fear. Many very talented people cannot work in this kind of atmosphere. Beyond that, many groups in our world today are formed to deal with complex problems requiring many different skill sets. Solving problems of this sort requires a high degree of collaboration. Under this model, collaboration can be very difficult.

I believe the orchestra is a better model for most organizations:

While not a perfect metaphor, it does have many advantages. Every member of the orchestra is important. Everyone is necessary. Each person is unique, and all are required. When they all play together from the same sheet music, in harmony, they produce beautiful sounds. Of course, even in the orchestra, there's a hierarchy. Generally, the first violin has the most status. But all of the various instruments have their special role and therefore may take pride in their special contribution. Even the triangle has a note to play!

I am told, in the era of our successful attempt to put a man on the moon, that JFK approached a man at Cape Canaveral who was sweeping the sidewalk and asked him politely, "And what are you doing?" Allegedly, the man answered, "Why, I'm helping to put a man on the moon." Yes, even the triangle has a note to play.

A NOTE ON SUBCULTURES

A good leader must work around the year, around the clock, on the culture of the entire organization, to make sure that the organization as a whole is focused on the big picture. If the organization's primary constituency is the *customer*, the leadership must daily reinforce the culture that keeps the entire organization focused on the customer. Otherwise, dangerous subcultures will begin to develop and will sabotage the leadership's effort to keep the organization focused on the main constituency, the customer.

Subcultures can arise in at least three different ways.

The most common type emerges when a manager, usually an inexperienced one, goes into the "heart of darkness." By that, I mean the manager sets up his/her kingdom, apart from that of the corporation, and builds a culture of his/her own. Often, first-time managers form a bond with their team that's based on mutual support. As opposed to bonding with his/her fellow managers, the first-time manager prioritizes allegiance to his team over allegiance to his fellow managers, i.e., over allegiance to the rest of the corporation. He creates an implicit contract with his team members: "If you support me, I will support you." To an extent, that's what every manager does. But, pushed by an inexperienced manager to an extreme, it begins to look like this: "You and I are better than the rest. If you tell all the employees that I am better than the other managers, I will tell the other managers that you are better than all the other employees." Soon, this "superior" little tribe begins to develop its own culture and often begins to run roughshod over other teams. Years ago, under our first CEO, we had three such managers. As their subcultures evolved, they became very protective of both themselves and the information they either held or generated. Trying to get information from their people or simply trying to work collaboratively with them became, in time, like making a foray into enemy territory. In fact, one of the three actually forbade employees who worked in other divisions from entering his part of the building without special permission. In time, they all left and were replaced by more mature managers who put the needs of the corporation above those of their individual tribes.

Other times, subcultures arise in distant places. The corporation grows and expands, and eventually sets up branches. At first, and especially if the managers are less mature as managers, we see the appearance of the "headquarters" syndrome. From the point of view of the branches, the headquarters doesn't understand the unique conditions under which the branches operate. The headquarters creates policies and takes measures that make it impossible for the branches to succeed. From the headquarters' viewpoint, the branches have "gone native." They're self-centered and think only of their own best interest, not really caring about the corporation's success as a whole. Soon, the branches have their own culture, one central tenet being the right to rebel against headquarters. Sadly, the headquarters culture evolves as well, to include a new tenet: The branches are like rebellious colonies. We must send in troops to keep them in line.

Sending in troops, as it turns out, only makes the situation worse. Actually, there's only one real answer. The branch manager must be pulled into the corporation as a whole. He must be encouraged to bond with his fellow managers from headquarters, and they must also be encouraged to bond with him. The CEO *must* go out of his/her way to make sure that the heads of the branches are never positioned as, or perceived to be, in a subordinate position relative to their peer managers at the headquarters. The CEO *must also* not allow the branch manager to act as if he had the right not to cooperate with his peers at the headquarters. At the same time, the branch manager must be capable of articulating the legitimate needs of his division, to the extent that they require exceptions, and the CEO must respect them. If the branch manager becomes the branch manager that we want him to become, the headquarters syndrome/branch rebellion problem will take care of itself. If not, the branch manager has to go.

Finally, a subculture may arise when a company hires a number of people from *another* company *all at the same time.*

Once, many years ago, we made the decision to expand our marketing department in one quantum leap, rather than ratably over time. That, in and of itself, was foolish. Even more foolishly, we hired all of our new recruits from the same company. They brought their own culture and firmly believed it was better than ours. It took years for this problem to dissipate. In the meantime, most of this new group's accomplishments were overshadowed by the problems they caused for the rest of us through their superior attitude, lack of interest in assimilation, and refusal to compromise.

Ask yourself:

→ What are the six to eight key values reflected in the culture of my company, unit, or team?

→ How would others in my company, unit, or team describe the culture they experience?

→ To what extent does this culture reflect my values and the values I want my team members to emulate?

→ What discrepancies exist between the values I espouse and the culture we now have?

→ What needs to change to get or keep them aligned?

→ What kind of person am I? What are my values? What values would I like my team to emulate?

→ How will I use my answers to the three questions above to build a culture in my organization?

→ Does everyone in my organization know what it means to be a member of my team, and whether they belong?

→ Does my organization operate on a horizontal or vertical basis?

→ How will I work on assembling and engaging cross-functional teams?

→ Do I take responsibility for all of my actions and decisions? Does everyone in my organization do the same?

→ Do I have any problems with subcultures in my organization? What will I do to improve the situation?

→ Do I have a "dogsled" or an "orchestra" culture in my organization? Is that what I want? If not, what will I do to change it?

BUILDING TRUST IN YOUR TEAM

*"Glass, China, and Reputation are easily crack'd,
and never well mended."*[19]

BENJAMIN FRANKLIN

Years ago, our company went through a nearly total management turnover. Within a year, we had an almost completely new management team. Only a few managers, myself included, remained from before the change. The new managers all came from different places and had very different ideas about how to run a bank. To further complicate matters, each of us thought we were right. And because we'd never worked together as a team, we lacked a well-recognized set of conventions for interacting with each other. Layer on a new CEO who trended, in various ways, toward creating a relatively politicized environment, and you had a perfect storm in the making. A profound lack of trust reigned among us.

A group of people who trust each other will get a lot more done than people who don't. So, what causes people to trust or mistrust each other?

Here's an example from my professional life. We hired an absolutely brilliant man. He had perhaps the fastest mind I've spent time with. And his values corresponded almost identically to those of the culture we were cultivating. What wasn't to like?

Unfortunately, it was extremely difficult to integrate him into the team, even though he was so smart that I really wanted to. What threw it all out of kilter was that his abundance of mental octane resulted in overthinking. If you asked him the time, he'd build you a clock. Plus, for reasons unfathomable, underneath it all, he was tremendously insecure and easily hurt. So, unfortunately, he became really defensive in situations in which he perceived himself

---

19 Benjamin Franklin, from *Poor Richard's Almanack*, 1753, Franklin Institute, accessed April 9, 2018, fi.edu/benjamin-franklin/famous-quotes.

to be under attack. He'd suddenly flip and shoot past the tipping point. In the middle of a management team meeting, for instance, he'd occasionally lash out and accuse everyone of hating and ostracizing him. People around the table were baffled by it. Since a large part of a team's success is trust and a willingness to rely on others' expertise, a single outburst like that can cause people to not want to be around you, much less want to rely on your expertise.

Trust within a management team makes it more successful. Trust makes us more efficient and effective, creating a more pleasant atmosphere, so when we wake up in the morning, we look forward to the day. It increases energy and enthusiasm. Trust is a primary characteristic of great organizations—in the management team and, by extension, permeating the entire organization.

America's Founding Fathers understood the importance of trust and reputation. So when they needed someone to represent the American colonies in France, they sent Benjamin Franklin. In 1776, Franklin arrived in Paris as America's first foreign ambassador to France, seeking aid for the American Revolution. As a celebrated scientist, statesman, inventor, writer, publisher, and philanthropist, his reputation preceded him. A kind of "Franklin fever" swept the city. Franklin fascinated people from all walks of life. But most important, they trusted him based on his lifetime of authenticity and good faith. In the end, Benjamin Franklin (along with John Adams and John Jay) successfully negotiated to secure French aid for the American colonies, building a valuable alliance that empowered the American Revolution and helped change the course of history.[20]

So, how do you generate and grow trust? We studied that for years at SVB, concluding that groups can talk about how to do it, but only individuals can put the ball into play. We generated the following list of "The Magic 12" ways to create and cultivate an atmosphere of trust within a circle of colleagues. If you succeed,

---

20 Library of Congress, *Benjamin Franklin: In His Own Words, Treaty of Paris*, accessed April 9, 2018, https://www.loc.gov/exhibits/franklin/franklin-treaty.html; Rick Adams, "Benjamin Franklin: The Original Hipster," The Franklin Institute, accessed April 11, 2018, fi.edu.

this circle of trust will, in time, spread to the entire organization. When it does, everyone will feel safer, be happier, and work more effectively.[21]

Please be aware: These look easy. In practice, they're harder than they look.

THE MAGIC 12

1. **Express yourself clearly and often.** Say what you think. Although it's unfair, introverts can have a harder time being trusted than extroverts. When people don't know what you're thinking, their ability to trust you diminishes. So, let others know what you think. Express your ideas with enough humility that you don't intimidate people into silence. Show genuine interest in the ideas of others. Never tell them they're wrong. Of course, it's fair to say that you see it differently, but that you're grateful that they're willing to tell you what they think. Encourage people to approach discussions with others displaying this same attitude.

2. **Be consistent.** Say the same thing every time you speak. Don't contradict yourself. In that way, you'll become predictable. Even if people disagree with your opinion, your predictability will engender trust. If you change your mind, don't just express a new opinion; tell people clearly and openly that you've changed your mind. If you say one thing on Monday and another on Tuesday, people will wonder if they can trust you. Be consistent. Expect others to follow this same procedure. Additionally, if anyone says something to one person, and something that appears to be totally different to another person, sooner or later these

---

21 Stephen M. R. Covey, *The Speed of Trust* (New York: Free Press, 2018), 129–241. Covey lists thirteen behaviors that generate trust, in comparison to my twelve, although there is, of course, some overlap.

two other people will compare notes. They'll both conclude that the first person cannot be trusted.

3. **Solicit opinions.** Ask someone's opinion and three things will happen: 1) they'll think you're smarter than they would otherwise, 2) they'll like you, and 3) they'll trust you. Ask often, ask regularly, ask sincerely. Express genuine interest. You can always learn from others. Learning from others does not mean that you have to take on their point of view completely, or even at all. Others will trust you more if you're genuinely interested in their views, even if you, in the end, still don't agree with them.

4. **Demonstrate respect.** Don't tell people they're wrong. Even if you disagree, don't tell them they're wrong. At the very least, compliment them on sharing an opinion that you find interesting and that you'd like to think about more. Remember, you can learn from opinions you disagree with. People will respect you for respecting them. And if they respect you, they'll trust you.

5. **Assume innocence.** Don't demonize those with whom you disagree. If you assume innocence, even disagreement can breed trust. If you demonize your enemies, even friends will lose their trust in you.

6. **Skip the agenda.** Try as often as possible to have a "conversation without an agenda." This is hard to understand at first, so please hear me out. If you can pull it off, it will generate more trust than almost anything else you can do. Most of the time, we hold "conversations with an agenda," even when we purport to be doing otherwise. When we ask others what they think, we're in most cases really creating a springboard from which we can tell them our opinion and hopefully bring them over to our side.

Example:

Husband: Honey, there are three movies, A, B, and C. Which would you rather see?

Wife: I think I'd like to see B.

Husband: B isn't as good as C. Let's see C.

Better would be:

"That's interesting. Why would you like to see B? I'd really like to understand your point of view. I'd thought that C might be better, but maybe I'm wrong."

Try to go through an entire conversation without defending your own point of view. Concentrate exclusively on trying to understand the other's viewpoint. You don't lose anything by doing so. But you gain a lot: the other person's trust. All I've asked you to do is postpone, not give up. Put your opinion on the shelf and leave it there for later. If, after the agenda-less conversation, you want your old opinion back again, you can have it. It's right there on the shelf, where you left it. Don't worry! It's yours for the taking. On the other hand, if you don't have a genuine interest in other people's opinions, you'll never learn anything that you didn't already know. Unless you're a genius, you'll fail. No, even if you're a genius, you'll fail. Even geniuses are wrong some of the time.

7. **Demonstrate relevant vulnerability.** When you're in doubt, admit it. Don't try to seem infallible. Admit when you're wrong. Don't wait for others to make you admit it. If you can follow this very simple, but very difficult-to-implement guideline, others will respect and trust you. Most people hate admitting they're wrong. Learn how to do it. Do it often. You'll soon realize it's not that hard to do. You lose nothing by doing it. On the contrary, you gain tremendously. At the

very least, people will respect you. Some may even love you for it.

8. **Let others decide.** You don't have to make every decision yourself. In fact, if you do, you'll deny your employees and team members the opportunity to practice decision-making within parameters. If you make every decision, people will either resent you or—worse—you'll find over time that you have a collection of employees and team members who are incapable of making decisions and are therefore nonpromotable. Even if they make a bad decision, if you've set appropriate parameters, you're better off than you would be if you had a whole collection of essentially nonpromotable people working for you. Also, if you let them make some decisions, they'll trust you. People trust others whom they perceive to trust them.

9. **Show support.** Support other people's decisions, even if they're below (rather than above) you in the pecking order. People trust those who support the decisions they've made. Over the long haul, trust is much more important than "perfect" decisions.

10. **Hire adults.** Avoid the extreme points on the spectrum of human behavior. Act like an adult, and treat others like adults. People don't trust those who are passive-aggressive (once they figure out who they are) or obnoxiously assertive. They trust adults who act like adults and treat others like adults.

11. **Control your inner demons.** We all have inner demons that rise up and try to control us when we're feeling insecure. If you can't control your inner demons, it will be hard for others to trust you. In the example I used a few pages ago, about the man with the computer-like brain, the "inner

demon" was insecurity. Insecurity drove him to over-explain and to feel "dissed" when others disagreed. If he had recognized his inner demon, he could have controlled it.

12. Observe the "9th Guiding Principle" (see description below).

THE 9th GUIDING PRINCIPLE

Years ago, our second CEO introduced the "8 Guiding Principles," a list of the kinds of lofty principles you'll find framed and hanging in the lobby of many US companies. None of us could remember them. Finally, an employee came up with the so-called 9th Guiding Principle, and it ended up being the only one we could consistently remember:

> "If you have an issue with another colleague,
> talk to him or her about it directly;
> do not discuss it with third parties."

We later amended this to allow a third-party discussion if you need coaching on how to address an issue with the person in question, but *only* if you actually go on to discuss it with that person. Talking to a third person to denigrate someone you have an issue with is *not* allowed. We all agreed that if called on to be a coach, we had to insist that the advice seeker use our coaching at the first opportunity to deal directly with the issue, with the person he or she had the issue with. If everyone adhered to the 9th Guiding Principle, trust would abound.

INVITE OTHERS TO JOIN YOU IN DEVELOPING YOUR THOUGHTS

Finally, I'd like to recommend a way of doing things that I've always found extremely effective. You may not, but I certainly do.

It has to do with how I go about developing my thoughts. It looks like this:

When grappling with a problem, I may spend the better part of several days thinking about it. But I spend most of that "thinking" time in conversation with others, either individually or in small groups of two or three, not alone by myself in my office. I keep lots of flip charts in my office and record my thought process as it evolves over time. For example, I'll bring in Bob, who's pretty smart and knows a lot about the topic in question. I'll describe the problem, often pictorially, and almost always using flip charts. I'll ask his opinion on various aspects of the problem. I'll write his opinion down on one of the flip charts. After our conversation, when Bob has left the room, I'll look at the flip charts and ruminate. I'll reformulate my own theory (point of view), based on Bob's input and my digesting/processing of his input. Later in the day, I'll invite Sharon to come spend some time with me. I'll do the same things again. In the course of the next several days, I'll do the same thing with various others. In a matter of days, I've developed a point of view of my own that's much closer to a real solution than my original viewpoint before starting this process.

This approach has several advantages:

1. I enjoy it.

2. I learn a lot.

3. My "final" point of view is much more sophisticated than my original one.

4. The people I involve in the process enjoy it as well.

5. They feel respected and appreciated.

6. To a certain extent, I've already achieved buy-in for whatever I decide in the end because they (whose buy-in I will ultimately seek) had input into the finished product, and they know it.

7. This approach builds trust among the members of your leadership team.

It is important to note that all groups have a culture, whether they know it or not. And some cultures are better than others. Good cultures produce better results. "Bad" cultures invariably, over time, produce sub-optimal results. Consider Uber, the ride-hailing company that competes with Lyft. Under the founding CEO, Travis Kalanick, Uber developed a culture that was well defined, but counterproductive. To explore, read Mike Isaac's article "How Uber Got Lost" in the *New York Times*, August 8, 2019.

To help define an effective work culture, consider these questions with your colleagues:

1. Do the people in your organization know "what it means to work there"?

2. Do they know and understand the significance of your organization's values?

3. Do you depend on a "cops and robbers" mechanism to ensure proper behavior, or do you attempt to instill in each of your people a "voice of the conscience"? Does your leadership motivate through fear or encouragement?

4. Are you more "vertical" or "horizontal"? That is, do you and your colleagues spend more time managing up and down, or do you spend more time managing sideways (building working relationships with peers)?

5. Do you and your colleagues deal with disagreement in an adult-to-adult fashion, or do you vacillate between being obnoxiously assertive and passive-aggressive?

6. Is your organization more like a dogsled or an orchestra?

7. Do you have subcultures? Are they productive or destructive? How do you deal with them?

8. How high is the level of trust in your organization, and what could you do to improve it?

Ask yourself:

→ Do the people in my organization trust each other?

→ How will I use the "Magic 12" ways to create and cultivate an atmosphere of trust in my organization?

→ Do I demonstrate respect and solicit other people's opinions?

→ How will I use the 9th Guiding Principle to improve trust and the culture throughout my organization?

"Courage! Do not fall back; in a little the place will be yours."
JOAN OF ARC

CHAPTER 4

GETTING EVERYONE POINTED IN THE RIGHT DIRECTION

"The Vision Thing"

This chapter talks about how to get everybody in your organization aligned with respect to where you want to go and how you want to get there. It answers the following questions:

→ What do we mean by values? What role do they play?

→ What do we mean by purpose? Who determines it?

→ What do we mean by vision, and who is responsible for it?

→ What is strategy and who formulates it?

→ What role do tactics play, and who determines them?

One of history's most unlikely and extraordinary heroines was Joan of Arc. She rallied the demoralized French Army, personally leading the troops into battle after victorious battle as they fought back the invading English, who were on the verge of conquering France. This teenage girl from a small rural town unswervingly followed her vision, which she said was divine, and convinced many thousands to do the same. Utilizing values, purpose, vision, strategy, and tactics, Joan bravely led the French Army to victory. She succeeded in her quest to rout the English, crown the displaced French dauphin as king, and restore the independence of France. Joan led by example, with courage and integrity, right to the end.

Any organization—whether it's an army, business, or nonprofit foundation—is a community. To get things done, it needs much more than an inspiring leader and a determined top management team. It needs values, purpose, vision, strategy, and tactics. Getting the entire organization pointed in the right direction means giving team members a clear understanding of each.

VALUES

Values are shared norms. They act as a North Star, enabling a group of people to know, in most cases intuitively, if at any given time they're pointed in the right direction. Values provide a context within which we make decisions about what we do and how we do it. Typically, values change very little over time. Initially, at least, they're the product of the top leader. He or she sets the tone. The leader decides whether the organization will be client-focused, whether it will always act ethically, and whether it will foster internal as well as external competition. The leader decides, even if half-consciously, how team members will treat each other through the way he or she treats others in the organization.

Over time, these values grow organically to become the foundation of your organizational culture. Team members copy their leaders' behaviors to such an extent that those behaviors become *norms.* Once they become norms, they continue to reinforce themselves. Team members who are comfortable with these behaviors stay and attract other people like themselves. Team members who are uncomfortable with these behaviors will self-select themselves out. They will leave, often of their own accord. In many cases they'll go off and form their own organizations, often selling the same product or service to the same target market, only driven by a different set of norms. At SVB, we inadvertently spawned a series of companies selling the same products and services to our same target market. The only significant difference was in their *values.* The people who left did so because they wanted a different culture. Ultimately, some cultures are better than others. Some win, while others lose. Culture may start as the leader's personal choice, but it will ultimately decide the entire organization's fate.

PURPOSE

If culture is about how an organization will behave internally and externally, then purpose is about what it wants to accomplish over the long haul. Why does it exist as an organization? Like culture, the purpose is usually set by the leader, but generally in consultation with others: the board, the management team, at least indirectly the market, etc. Think of purpose as a destination. *Where* do we want to be in twenty-five years, and *who* do we want to be in twenty-five years?

Like values and culture, "purpose" functions like a North Star. It allows us to know at any given time whether we're pointed the right way, or whether a decision we're about to make will keep us on course or take us in a new direction. But where culture is about how we treat each other, purpose addresses our future goals. For example, SVB's purpose is to be "the premier provider of innovative financial services to entrepreneurial companies of all sizes worldwide."

VISION

What will your organization and the world in which it operates look like when the purpose has been achieved? It's no accident that I've used a word here that describes "seeing." Your team members and other constituencies expect leaders to paint a picture of what their lives will be like when you and your organization have arrived in the "promised land." The more graphic you can make that picture, the better. *Many top leaders fall short here because they fail to appreciate how important it is for people to be able to see, in their mind's eye, the world and their role in it. If you can paint a picture that's vivid and compelling in their eyes, they'll follow you toward it.* You, as the leader, can do everything else right, but if you fail to create and regularly articulate a vision, you may never be able to inspire your troops to realize their potential.

Joan of Arc, for example, was a master at using simple language and vivid imagery to paint a clear picture for her troops so they could visualize the English menace and the importance of battles to come. She also used this kind of speech to warn the enemy of what would befall them if they failed to comply with her demands, as shown in the letter she sent before the Siege of Orleans:

> *King of England, and you Duke of Bedford, calling yourself regent of France . . . do right in the King of Heaven's sight. [Surrender to the Maid] sent hither by God the King of Heaven, the keys of all the good towns you have taken and laid waste in France. . . . If you do not, expect to hear tidings from The Maid who will shortly come upon you to your very great hurt. And to you, King of England, if you do not thus, I am "chief de guerre"; and whenever I meet your followers in France, I will drive them out; if they will not obey, I will put them all to death. . . . If they obey, I will show them mercy. Do not think otherwise; you will not withhold the kingdom of France. . . . If you do not believe these tidings from God and The Maid, wherever we find*

you we shall strike you and make a greater tumult ["hahay"]
than France has heard for a thousand years. . . .You Duke of
Bedford, The Maid prays and beseeches not to bring yourself to
destruction. If you obey her, you may join her company, where
the French shall do the fairest deed ever done for Christendom.
Answer, if you desire peace in the city of Orleans; if not, bethink
you of your great hurt soon.[22]

Unsatisfied with the enemy's response, Joan sent a follow-up
letter:

You men of England, who have no right to this Kingdom of
France, the King of Heaven orders and commands you through
me, Joan the Pucelle, to abandon your strongholds and go back
to your country. If not, I will make a war cry ["hahu"] that will
be remembered forever. And I am writing this to you for the third
and final time; I will not write anything further.

As Father Jean Pasquerel later testified, "She took an arrow, tied
the letter with a thread to the tip and told an archer to fire this
arrow at the English," shouting, "'Read, this is news!'"[23]

I'd like to say more about vision because this, more than any of
the other concepts, presents a stumbling block for many leaders.
First, a few more examples from history: Genghis Khan, Christopher
Columbus, Moses, and President Ronald Reagan. Each in his own
way painted a picture with words for his followers of how glorious
life would be if they realized their vision.

---

22 Kathryn Harrison, *Joan of Arc* (New York: Doubleday, a division of Random House, 2014), 123–124.

23 Harrison, *Joan of Arc*, 150.

Consider the following:

Genghis Khan:

"The greatest happiness is to vanquish your enemies, to chase them before you, to rob them of their wealth, to see those dear to them bathed in tears. . ."[24]

Christopher Columbus:

"But in truth, should I meet with gold or spices in great quantity, I shall remain till I collect as much as possible, and for this purpose I am proceeding solely in quest of them."[25]

Moses:

"And I have said, I will bring you up out of the affliction of Egypt unto the land of the Canaanites, and the Hittites, and the Amorites, and the Perizzites, and the Hivites, and the Jebusites, unto a land flowing with milk and honey."[26]

Ronald Reagan:

"So, let us ask ourselves, 'What kind of people do we think we are?' And let us answer, 'Free people, worthy of freedom and determined not only to remain so but to help others gain their freedom as well.'"[27]

What do all of these visions have in common? First, they create a picture in the mind's eye. Second, they are lofty. Third, they are desirable from the point of view of the followers, not just the leaders.

And fourth, which is not necessarily obvious from the content of the quotes themselves, they are repeatable. I can imagine each of these four leaders repeating their respective quote often, perhaps at

---

24 Attributed to Genghis Khan, Goodreads, accessed October 14, 2018, goodreads.com.

25 Attributed to Christopher Columbus, BrainyQuote, accessed October 14, 2018, brainyquote.com.

26 Moses, Exodus 3:17, *King James Bible*, accessed October 14, 2018, biblehub.com.

27 Ronald W. Reagan, *Address to Members of the British Parliament, June 8, 1982*, accessed October 14, 2018, heritage.org.

the beginning of speeches, each time they addressed their troops, much like a liturgy.

So, why do so many leaders neglect to present a vision to their followers? I've pondered this for years. I think there are three potential reasons. First, some leaders just don't have the imagination needed to develop a vision. They got to where they are by being either tacticians or strategists, but not visionaries. Second, many leaders feel silly articulating a vision. They mistakenly believe that visions are for poets and prophets, not for leaders, to articulate. Finally, some leaders just get lazy over time. They lack the discipline necessary to regularly articulate the vision.

A case in point: During George H. W. Bush's entire four-year presidency, he was dogged by "the vision thing" (his own wording).[28] Some would say that it resulted in his not getting reelected to a second term. In any case, and for whatever reason, he felt uncomfortable with the idea of "articulating a vision." Many felt that he had one, perhaps even a very good one. Others felt that he had no grand dream. Both critics and admirers felt that he failed at "the vision thing."

Without a vision to focus and inspire them, followers will eventually lose heart.

STRATEGY

As opposed to culture and purpose, strategy is about how we'll get to our destination. If purpose is the endpoint, and vision what the endpoint will actually look like, and culture the rules of the road, then strategy is the road map itself. It's the route we'll take to get there. While culture, purpose, and vision don't change much over time, strategy can and *must* change in response to changes in the market and the world around us. In sailing, if the winds shift but our destination stays the same, we may need to adjust our sails and tack; this is tantamount to adjusting our strategy.

---

28 The elder Bush was dogged by what he referred to as "the vision thing" throughout his presidency. There are numerous articles online describing his struggle with "vision."

Who determines strategy? Many people contribute to its development. In a corporation, for example, this could include upper-level executives, mid-tier management, the board, and sometimes external consultants. The CEO is ultimately responsible for the strategy. However, if the CEO is doing his/her job properly, many will have contributed to its formulation and ongoing reformulation.

A word on the distinction between strategy and culture and their relative importance. I think I've said only one thing in my life that may actually be quotable: "Culture trumps strategy." An organization's two most important aspects are its strategy (long-term game plan) and culture (how the people in the corporation work together to effect the strategy). Many corporations devote too much attention to strategy and not enough to culture. The bottom line: If you have a great culture but a so-so strategy, your team will figure out how to improve the strategy. But if you have a great strategy and a so-so culture, you probably won't succeed. Even a great strategy can't compensate for an inferior culture.

TACTICS

The final layer, tactics, is all about the little decisions we make along a journey: Where to stop for the night, what supplies to buy, the best way to change a tire or mend a sail, etc. All these decisions will be made within the context of the culture, purpose, and strategy, and—if the leader is doing his or her job properly—*by the people actually implementing the decisions.* Unlike culture and purpose, which almost never change, and unlike strategy, which changes only from time to time, tactics can and should change regularly as we discover more effective ways of moving forward.

To accomplish anything, a complex organization must have values, purpose, vision, strategy, and tactics in place. Leaders are *responsible* for all of these things, but they cannot create them alone.

Each concept has an inherently different time horizon. A purpose might never change, or if it does, it only happens at pivotal points in an organization's evolution. The vision might change if and when the purpose changes, which might be never, but you'll constantly be refining (as opposed to changing) it. A well-conceived strategy will last at least three to five years, although it may need ongoing refinement. Tactics change most frequently as people learn how to do things better, or as better information becomes available. Values, as I've said before, rarely change. They may evolve in some respects, but they almost never change completely.

WHO DOES WHAT?

Since an organization's values, purpose, vision, strategy, and tactics are critical to achieving organizational alignment, it's important to know who owns, influences, or is responsible for each.

→ The CEO is responsible for **culture**.

→ The CEO, with input from the management team and with the board's approval, is responsible for determining the **purpose**.

→ It is always the CEO who creates and articulates the **vision**.

→ The management team, employees, and board will expect the CEO to take responsibility for creating and articulating the **vision**. The CEO who does the best job of creating and articulating the vision will be the most successful.

→ The CEO and management team are responsible for creating the **strategy**. The board is responsible for approving it.

→ The employees are responsible for creating the **tactics**. In fact, if we don't leave the tactics up to the employees, they will be unhappy and unmotivated.

Letting Go and Allowing Others to Determine HOW the Strategy Is Carried Out

If you can't let go, you shouldn't be a leader. Only people who know how to let go can lead successfully. Great leaders articulate the vision. They work with their teams to create the strategy. But they leave the execution of the strategy to the managers and the people who report to the managers.

Earlier in my career, I was for a time in charge of a subsidiary, complete with its own purpose, vision, strategy, values, and tactics. After I left that subsidiary, my successor—who understood strategy and tactics but wasn't tuned in to purpose, vision, or culture—faced obstacles. Ultimately, his fundamental lack of understanding about these concepts and how to work with them kept him from the success he might otherwise have enjoyed. He talked often about strategy, which is good, but he also talked about tactics and wanted to decide on them himself. Employees rejected this. First, his obsession with tactics caused them to lose respect for him; a true leader leaves tactics to others. Second, it caused them to feel that he didn't trust them because tactics were their domain. Why would he do their job for them if he really trusted them? they wondered. The leader's lack of vision left them uninspired, and because he failed to reinforce the culture, the values (that together make up the culture) fell slowly by the wayside. In time, employees lost their sense of what it meant to work there. They felt lost and disoriented.

Remember, the CEO determines the values. In doing so, he/she builds the culture. The CEO sets the tone, and the rest of the company follows suit.

Just as important, the CEO articulates the vision. If he/she fails to articulate the vision, the organization will lack direction and motivation.

Let me end with a concrete example, taken directly from my experience at SVB:

When I became CEO in April of 2001, the strategy that we had been pursuing since our founding in 1983 had exhausted itself. Our first CEO had always talked about his "three-legged-stool strategy." By that, he meant we had three target markets: 1) early-stage technology companies, 2) small real estate developers, and 3) Main Street USA (everybody else, as long as they weren't too big for us). From 1990 to 1992, the real estate part had gotten us into trouble, which resulted in our first CEO leaving and our second CEO coming on board. Our second CEO shrank the real estate from 33 percent to about 20 percent, shrank the tech part from 33 percent to about 20 percent, and increased the Main Street part from 33 percent to about 60 percent. Further, he took that 60 percent and divided it into "niches." We moved from cultivating a reputation as a "tech bank" to cultivating a reputation as a "niche bank." By 2001, nearly every one of our niches was in trouble, including tech. However, what made tech different from everything else we did was the following: It was the only area in which we had expertise that no one else had. When it came to real estate or Main Street, we were just one of 8,000 to 10,000 banks, with no particular advantages that set us apart. However, with respect to tech, we were number one, out of 8,000 to 10,000, particularly with respect to early-stage lending, which is a category of lending that is totally different from all others practiced by all the other banks.

With this as the backdrop, here is what we did under my leadership:

We have ourselves a new purpose:
to become the premier provider of innovative financial services
to entrepreneurial companies of all sizes worldwide.

This new purpose pointed us in a brand-new direction in three different ways.

→ First, we wanted to provide innovative financial services *of all types*, not just traditional commercial banking.

→ Second, we wanted to address the needs of entrepreneurial companies *of all sizes*, not just start-ups.

→ Third, we wanted to work with entrepreneurial companies of all sizes *worldwide*, not just in the US.

As the CEO, I was responsible for this new purpose, and for the three important changes that it involved. Of course, I worked with the board, with some external consultants, and with the senior management team to develop this purpose. The change in purpose was a *big* one. It involved taking tech from 20 percent of our business to 100 percent of our business. (In reality, to 99.5 percent of our business, in that we kept one of our old niches from before—namely, boutique wineries.) It involved spending hundreds of millions of dollars (over time) to invest in innovative products that would enable us to go beyond simply commercial banking, to accommodate the needs of very large tech companies and not just start-ups, and to enable us to work with companies in every major center of innovation around the world.

I should also point out that a few members of our senior management team were so uncomfortable with these changes that they made the decision to leave the organization. Whenever you make *really big* decisions like these, the senior management team will end up dividing itself into three categories: those who agree, those who don't agree but are willing to commit to supporting the new direction anyway, and those who cannot agree and will have to leave.

As I look back on my tenure, I made only about three big decisions the whole time I was CEO, and those were the ones described above. Beyond these three decisions, I focused on developing the values and the culture, and on creating and articulating the vision. In other words, I focused on *purpose, culture,* and *vision*.

I left strategy to the senior management team. And I insisted that they leave tactics to all of the hundreds of people who reported to them.

At the other end of the line of authority, our amazingly good chairman's approach was similar to the one that I took vis-à-vis the people who reported to me. Specifically, Pete Hart delegated, almost to an extreme. And I loved it. His view was that the board was there to: 1) make sure that nobody broke the law, and 2) offer me advice. That said, his view was that I didn't have to take any of the advice that he gave me. On the other hand, as he from time to time pointed out, the board could always fire me if they felt that too many of my decisions were bad ones. For me, perfect! I got excellent advice, I got to make my own decisions, and I enjoyed full responsibility for whether or not they were good ones.

This approach served us well. In addition to enabling our bank to get through the "valley of the shadow of death" that started with the dot-com meltdown of 2001 and lasted through the overall meltdown of 2008 virtually unscathed, this approach laid the foundation for the truly amazing success that the bank has enjoyed under the leadership of my successor, Greg Becker, who has been in charge since I passed the baton to him in April of 2011.

Ask yourself:

→ How vivid and compelling is our organization's purpose and vision?

→ How effective and comfortable am I in articulating our purpose, vision, strategy, and values? What about my direct reports?

→ To what extent do our employees "see" our purpose and vision and reflect it in their day-to-day actions?

→ What can my team do to make our purpose and vision clearer and more striking?

→ Who owns, influences, or is responsible for determining values, purpose, vision, strategy, and tactics?

→ What do we need to do more or less of?

"Diversity in counsel, unity in command."
CYRUS THE GREAT

CHAPTER 5

MAKING AND EXECUTING ON GREAT DECISIONS

Cyrus the Great

This chapter talks about:

1. How, as the leader, to leverage yourself through others. You don't want to do everything yourself, and you don't want to make every decision yourself. Great leaders delegate most decisions to others. Great leaders inspire others to take responsibility and to solve problems.

2. How great leaders, with the support of their executive teams, make great decisions.

3. How great leaders help team members resolve conflict between themselves.

4. How great leaders hold effective meetings with their executive teams.

"People who work together will win,
whether it be against complex football defense
or the problems of modern society."[29]

VINCE LOMBARDI

THE LEADER AS COACH

You've chosen your team. With your team's input—augmented by appropriate input from and approval by key stakeholders—you've set the purpose and developed the strategy. You're ready to articulate your vision. You and your management team have delegated execution (tactics) to your employees. You know your values and are ready to walk them (demonstrate them through your leadership example) and talk them (describe them in writing and speeches). At this point, your main job is coaching your management team. The main job of your top executives and direct reports will be coaching *their* teams.

Coaching is a full-time job. Providing feedback on how well people are doing and ways they could be more effective is a large part of coaching. Effective feedback is frequent, immediate, and direct. This comes easily to many leaders. If it doesn't come easily to you, you must work on it until it does. "They call it coaching but it is teaching," said one of football's greatest coaches, Vince Lombardi. "You do not just tell them . . . you show them the reasons."[30]

I touched on this earlier, and it bears repeating. When you become a leader, your job is no longer the activity of the group that you're managing. If you're a football player who becomes a coach, you don't keep scrimmaging with the team on the field; you stay out of the active game and coach the players to help them improve and work better together. If you're a lender, you're no longer lending; you should be coaching the other lenders. If you're in an accounting

---

29 Lombardi, accessed April 9, 2018, www.vincelombardi.com/quotes.html.

30 Lombardi, accessed April 9, 2018, www.vincelombardi.com/quotes.html.

group and become the head of it, you should no longer be doing the actual accounting work yourself; you should be coaching. Where many people fail is thinking that as leaders they should be the best in the group at the actual activity. Coaching—managing anything—is totally different from doing the job itself. Some people can be the very best at accounting, for example, and still fail as coaches. Alternatively, you don't have to be the best accountant in the group to be the best coach. Two almost totally different jobs!

I've observed examples of this firsthand. Tom was great at lending. The volume and quantity of his work resulted in his manager recommending him for promotion: to lead another team of lenders. Like most people, Tom assumed that what got him promoted (the volume and quantity of his loans) was what he should focus on in his new job. He didn't realize that his new job was totally different. He was no longer a lender; he was now a manager. Managers coach others to succeed. Instead, Tom kept right on lending alongside the people who now reported to him. Over time, he failed as a manager. His direct reports felt that he was, in a sense, *competing with them*. Instead of finding Tom inspiring, they found him threatening. With no one to coach them and help them succeed, they felt ignored. The team failed. And because they failed, by definition Tom also failed, his own production notwithstanding.

In the end, it's important to have perspective about the larger picture in which you and your organization are operating. "After all the cheers have died down and the stadium is empty," Vince Lombardi said, "after the headlines have been written, and after you are back in the quiet of your room and the championship ring has been placed on the dresser and after all the pomp and fanfare have faded, the enduring thing that is left is the dedication to doing with our lives the very best we can to make the world a better place in which to live."[31]

---

31 Lombardi, accessed April 9, 2018, www.vincelombardi.com/quotes.html.

HOW GREAT LEADERS LEVERAGE
THEMSELVES THROUGH OTHERS

Some CEOs squander their positions of power by trying to do everything themselves. I imagine they do this because, in their passion to get things done and get them done right, they are *too anxious* to "get it right" to delegate work and decisions to others on their team. Unfortunately, by focusing on doing tasks themselves, they're missing the opportunity to leverage themselves through others. In other words, as the leader, I can focus on doing tasks myself, or I can focus on leveraging myself through others. The result? Instead of having just one person (myself) working on something, I could have eight other people (direct reports) working on it, which would free me up to think about the big picture. Thinking about the big picture is the job of the leader.

I remember a time, early in my career, when there were only six people in our office: the boss (Allyn), the other lender (Dave, one of my best friends), the office manager (Christine), two trainees (Frank and Andrea), and me. We had just broken loose from the failing Bank of New England and started the first branch of Silicon Valley Bank outside of Northern California, in Boston. We were so far away from California that we felt like we had a bank of our own, not just a branch of another bank. Quickly, Dave and I built up portfolios so large that we needed to hire people to help us. Soon, however, I noticed that Dave was getting ahead of me. His portfolio was growing larger than mine by the month. How? I wondered. So I decided to try to figure it out. It didn't take me long. Dave was delegating everything he could to the trainees we'd hired to help us. I wasn't. Dave understood leverage. I didn't.

Some CEOs think their job is to be the decider and/or the executor: the hero who saves the day. But good CEOs don't actually do that much. When they're not cultivating the culture, they spend their time coaching their team members who are not as experienced.

They coach others to do things rather than doing things themselves. By delegating to others in this way, CEOs are helping their team members do their jobs the best they can. They're also strengthening their workforce so team members will be better equipped to dive in and more independently handle the next situation that arises. They are preparing their team members for the future.

When I became CEO, one of my best board members took me aside. "Your job is now different from before," he said. "You should no longer be managing relationships with clients. Of course, you can assist, as appropriate. But you should be delegating the management of even important relationships to others, and then spend your time coaching. Only by coaching will you achieve leverage. Only if you learn to leverage yourself through others will the bank achieve success."

HOW GREAT LEADERS DELEGATE DECISION-MAKING TO OTHERS, EMPOWER OTHERS, AND TEACH OTHERS TO HONE THEIR DECISION-MAKING SKILLS

Every leader, every day, faces a multitude of potential decision-making events. I tend to group them into three categories:

1. Decisions that I should make myself *without* input from others. Typically, these are smaller decisions with less-consequential outcomes. I don't need advice or buy-in, and I don't want to delegate.

2. Decisions I'd like to delegate. This is far and away *the largest group.* I trust others and want them to be able to make decisions. I set the parameters commensurate with their purview and judgment. The broader their purview and the better their judgment, the wider the parameters. If I want people to learn in a way that will

help them take more responsibility in the future, I must allow (and in some cases, even force) them to make decisions within the broadest possible parameters.

3. The third and smallest category includes the really big decisions: those I need and want to make myself, but on which I would like input from others, to increase the quality of the decisions and to secure buy-in from people who report to me and other relevant stakeholders. In ten years as CEO, only a handful of decisions fit into this category.

Notice that in the second category, the people to whom I delegate decisions will need to do the same thing I did. They, too, will need to divide decisions into the three categories I used, and then proceed accordingly. In this way, decision-making will cascade down to the lowest level possible, as close to the client as it can be. The closer to the client that decisions are made, the better.

To the extent that I delegate decision-making to others, I need to mean it. I can tell them what I think, but I need to let them make their own decisions. I can't try to influence them unduly or force them in a specific direction. That said, I owe it to my direct reports to audit their decisions from time to time, to let them know what I think of their judgment. This is the only way they will learn. My perception of the quality of their decisions is an integral part of my perception of their performance. I owe it to them to give periodic feedback on their performance.

AUDITING THE DECISIONS YOU'VE DELEGATED: Feedback

Periodically, you'll need to evaluate your direct reports. Many leaders shy away from this or avoid it altogether. Here's my set of rules that I try to follow religiously. First, I try to formally (in writing) review my direct reports at least every six months. Second, I try to never put anything in writing that I haven't already discussed with them in the six months prior. This means I'm coaching them and providing feedback almost daily.

My reviews always consist of three parts:

→ What's going well,

→ What could go better, and

→ What steps to take to ensure that what could go better actually will go better.

This third part implies development. I believe that every leader, including myself, should always be working on a development plan. Leading is like golf: working on your swing is a lifelong undertaking.

As your direct reports improve *their* swing, it's important to recognize and reward that improvement. Exactly how you do so should be as much a function of that person's unique personality as of your own inclinations and tastes. Reward and recognition take many forms. Choose methods that are commensurate with the accomplishment and that also fit the recipient's personality.

Development is key: It's not enough to tell your direct reports what they do well and how they could be more effective. You must also help them develop themselves: Build on their strengths and shore up their weaknesses. Help them find the right job relative to their strengths, gain the skills they'll need, and develop the leadership traits and techniques that will make them successful. "Leaders are made, they are not born," Vince Lombardi said. "They are made by hard effort, which is the price which all of us must pay to achieve any goal that is worthwhile."[32]

Everyone wants to be successful, and there is a place for everyone. If it's not at your company, it may be at someone else's. It's your job to help each of your direct reports find the right fit.

---

32 Lombardi, accessed April 9, 2018, www.vincelombardi.com/quotes.html.

Here's how:

I've always found that when you want to give feedback about how to do things differently, it's best to acknowledge that you've made the same or similar mistakes yourself. There really are so many mistakes you can make along the way, and it's usually good to start with a combination of acknowledging, "I did this, too" or "I could have done that, too" and showing some empathy for what drove the person you're talking with to engage in that behavior. Then you're on their side. And consider that you probably don't know the person's family history. Often, children of authoritarian parents find even small criticisms devastating. Soften criticisms in any way you can. Occasionally, though, you'll run into people on the other end of the spectrum; you practically have to hit them over the head before they understand what you're talking about. You'll run into these people less frequently.

Maintaining Some Distance

If you're in charge, you just can't be close friends with everybody. You need to maintain some level of distance. At SVB, we teach a course called "Bud to Boss," which coaches newly minted leaders on how to make the transition from being someone's buddy to being somebody's boss. If you haven't had training on this subject or at least given it some serious thought, I suggest that you do.

An Example: Grooming My Successor

Most people don't believe me, but I actually picked my ultimate successor a full year *before* I became CEO. Greg joined SVB three years after I did. But I didn't really get to know him until I became chief banking officer, and that was three years before I became CEO. At that time, Greg was in charge of a newly formed branch in Boulder, Colorado. He was doing a terrific job. I admired the way he led his small band on the frontier.

A year or two later, I pulled him back to California, promoting him from head of a small office in Boulder to head of a major division on Sand Hill, in Menlo Park. The way he led that division proved to all concerned that I'd made the right decision in choosing him for the job.

Soon, I came to the conclusion that if I became CEO, I would groom him to be my successor. A year after reaching this conclusion, I was promoted to CEO.

More than any other member of my management team, Greg had opinions of his own that he was willing to defend. More than any other, Greg was willing to debate with me.

During my ten years as CEO, I made only a handful of *big* decisions. All the other big decisions I delegated to Greg and other members of the management team. From my point of view, most of the decisions Greg made during those ten years were good ones. He usually consulted with me, his peers, and his direct reports before making big decisions. A few times, I thought the decision he was about to make was *wrong*. When that happened, I told him so, and why. Sometimes he deferred to my "better judgment," sometimes he didn't. Sometimes it turned out that I was right. Sometimes he was right. In either case, I supported him. And in either case, it was Greg who made the decision because I'd delegated it to him to make. That's how Greg honed his judgment. That's, in part, what helped him become the excellent CEO he is today.

Ask yourself:

→ How effective and confident am I in performing my role as coach to my direct reports?

→ To what extent am I able to easily and effectively provide them with frequent, immediate, and direct feedback?

→ How am I doing when it comes to regular and beneficial evaluation, recognition, and rewards?

→ What will I do to improve in these areas?

→ What will I do to encourage my direct reports to develop their skills, including delegation?

HOW GREAT LEADERS MAKE BIG DECISIONS THEMSELVES WITH THE SUPPORT OF THEIR TEAMS

When leaders make *big* decisions, they should seek advice from others. "Others" should include stakeholders, people with relevant expertise, key members of their various constituencies, and members of their executive team.

Why? Because no matter how smart they are, they cannot know everything. Leaders who consult with others before making big decisions will almost always make better decisions. First, because they will learn from the expertise of others. Second, because their constituencies will feel that they are part of the process (*which they in fact are*) and will therefore find it easier to buy in to the outcome.

A word of warning: Consulting with others before making big decisions is not about voting. When I consult with others before making big decisions, it doesn't mean I am turning our company into a democracy. I occasionally even let people vote, but that doesn't mean I've abdicated my role as the ultimate decision-maker. It just means that, on occasion, I let people vote. If I decide when people are allowed to vote, it is hardly a democracy.

Consulting with others is at the heart of making great decisions. That said, in my experience, it is a rarity. Most people just aren't used to or comfortable with the idea of soliciting the opinions of others. Most, in my experience, are sole contributors. This is not the way to optimize talent. If we consult with the *right* other people, we accomplish so much more than we ever could alone.

What do I mean by the "right" people? At SVB, we went out of our way to hire intelligent people from culturally and professionally diverse backgrounds who knew how to work together. Years ago, we found that out of one thousand employees at the time, we had fifty-five first languages represented in our company. With that, fewer than 50 percent of the people we hired (for whom this was not their first job) came from within the banking industry. Instead, they'd had all sorts of other experiences. One person I personally hired grew into the biggest revenue generator in our history. Before joining us, he was a concierge at the Four Seasons hotel. "Right people" aren't always the ones with a four-page résumé in your particular field or industry.

Many years ago, I had a guy named Tim reporting to me. Tim was definitely the "command and control" type. In the end, he was a sole contributor, not the kind of person who naturally consults with others. He was, to put it bluntly, a "decider." One day, during our monthly one-on-one, Tim told me that he was planning to reorganize his division soon. I asked when. That very afternoon, he replied. When I asked with whom he'd consulted while formulating his plan, Tim said he'd planned it out all by himself. In other words, he hadn't gotten input from his boss (me), his colleagues (the other division managers), his lieutenants (his direct reports), or anyone in HR (the experts). I predicted the reorg would fail. Why? Because he hadn't availed himself of other people's advice, and in reality, no single manager is smart enough to foresee everything that could go wrong. Also, he was the only one with any stake in the outcome. Six months later, my prediction came true. The reorg failed. He had to undo it.

At the other end of the spectrum are managers who, rather than acting independently, pay too much attention to what others think. Ed, another manager I worked with around the same time as Tim, was planning a project within his division. To me, it seemed to be taking too long to finish. One day, Ed and I were on our way to a client call together. Ed was driving, and I used our time together for a one-on-one. I asked Ed how the project was going and why it was taking so long. Ed said he was ready but was held back by the lack of consensus among his lieutenants. I almost lost it. "What are you talking about?" I yelled (not a good leadership example on my part, I admit). Collaborative decision-making is not about getting consensus. If we wait for consensus, we'll never embark on anything. Consensus is, at best, accidental. My wife and I have been married for thirty-seven years, and we've never achieved consensus on anything except by coincidence, and then only occasionally.

Consensus building is not an effective decision-making practice. I don't believe it ever really exists, except by coincidence. Even if you could achieve consensus, it would take too long to get there.

When I make big decisions, I want to make the best choices possible. And I know that I can make better decisions if I get advice from others first. I can also get more buy-in from others if I ask for their advice.

However, no matter how long I wait, I know I will never achieve consensus. If I appear to, it is probably because someone is pretending just to make me happy.

The most effective organizations are not democracies. Nor, at the other end of the spectrum, should they be dictatorships. Leaders *must* listen to and consider the opinions and knowledge of those who report to them. They must listen to stakeholders and experts. Dictatorship results in sub-optimal decisions and revolt. Leaders may take a vote, on occasion, but companies are not democracies. Consensus is an illusion, as people only pretend to agree. People who wait for *real* consensus will wait forever. This leaves only what I like to call consultative decision-making: consulting with key stakeholders and relevant experts before making big decisions.

Consultative decision-making, as I define it, is perhaps best expressed in the words of the Persian king Cyrus the Great (600 BCE): "Diversity in counsel, unity in command." Using this quote as a starting point, we developed an approach at SVB called "The Four Ds" (described below), which I believe captures a basic methodology that's been followed by many of the greatest leaders in world history, and ignored—to their detriment—by many of the others.

THE FOUR Ds

"Diversity in counsel, unity in command."[33]

CYRUS THE GREAT[34]

When faced with a big decision at SVB, I would call together my direct reports—all members of our Steering Committee (called the Executive Committee in other companies). I'd explain the issue and ask for their advice. In other words, I'd seek to benefit from their collective intelligence and experience so I could make a *better* decision than I otherwise might.

To be clear about what I wanted, I'd begin by telling them one of the following:

1. I've already made a decision, this is what it is, and I want your advice on implementing it; *or*

2. I've already made a decision, this is what it is, and I want your opinion on whether or not it is a good one; *or*

3. I have a decision to make and I want your input; *or*

4. I have a decision to make, I want to discuss it with you, and then I'm going to have you vote on it; *or*

5. We have a decision to make, I'd like you to discuss it (perhaps even without me there), and then I'd like you to decide and let me know the outcome.

What I've just described is part of what we at SVB referred to as the "Four Ds" of decision-making: *Debate* (or discuss), *Decide, Deliver,* and *Debrief.*

---

33 There are numerous versions of "the three (or four, or even five) Ds of decision-making," although I know of none that are based on "Diversity in counsel, unity in command" (Cyrus the Great) and, correspondingly, none similar to my own. Check the Web.

34 Cyrus the Great, Goodreads, accessed June 18, 2018, https://www.goodreads.com.

Here's how the Four Ds work:

1. Debate

During the debate (or discuss) phase, everyone present is expected to participate. Those present should include both stakeholders and experts. People should express their views openly and directly, yet respectfully. Members of my management team are being paid to give us the benefit of their intelligence and knowledge. For them to withhold either, especially during this "debate" phase, would be to shirk their responsibility. Withholding is not acceptable, but neither is yelling, insulting, browbeating, or belittling.

The leader, in particular, must be acutely aware of his or her power, and must meticulously avoid intimidating group members by stating an opinion too early or emphatically. In most cases, the minute the leader expresses an opinion, the debate stops. Why? Because most employees, consciously or not, want to be in sync with the leader.

There's an art to knowing how long to debate or discuss. No two people will ever agree on how much is enough. The leader has to decide this for the group. Strive for just enough: not too little, not too much. Whoever is the decider should wait to make the decision until he/she is satisfied that all experts and stakeholders have expressed their view, *and* that he/she has understood what they've said.

2. Decide

Someone has to make a decision. Generally, it's clear who's responsible. Whoever is responsible must decide. The leader cannot abdicate responsibility. The leader can decide to ask for a vote, but he/she is still responsible. If the leader decides on a vote—and if the group votes on an outcome that's contrary to what he/she would do, and the leader decides to accept the will of the group—he/she is still responsible. The leader *cannot* blame an undesirable outcome on the group.

In any given situation, if it's unclear from the outset who the ultimate decider will be, it's essential to establish this as soon as possible. Usually, the highest-ranking person in the group either is the decider or decides who the decider is. If that doesn't work, then someone higher, outside the group, must make that determination. Not knowing who the ultimate decider will be can cause almost any group to flounder.

If all else fails, the CEO should either make the decision or decide who is to make the decision.

3. Deliver

The delivery phase means getting the work done. In this phase, we insist that everyone pitch in and help, regardless of how they felt or thought about the decision. It's okay to still disagree (no one can stop you, anyway), but it's no longer okay to voice it or to allow it to influence your willingness to help in the implementation. This is called "disagree but commit." Committing means helping to get it done. No one is allowed to "talk trash" or sabotage. We didn't go as far as George Washington, who hanged saboteurs, but we expected everyone to support the decision, or they needed to go.

It's also important to institutionalize processes and procedures that enable you to track and evaluate progress. If you expect people to execute, they need to understand the decision and all of its ramifications. And you need to measure results and hold people accountable.

In 2003 (or so), when SVB was in the process of changing our purpose, and accordingly, our strategy, we had considerable disagreement, particularly among members of the senior executive team. Some wanted to forge on ahead; others wanted to stay with our old purpose and continue to pursue the old strategy. It was tearing us apart. At that point, Greg and I went to visit with a professor in the Graduate School of Business at Stanford who had advised Intel when it was going through a change in purpose and strategy that was equally significant some years before. He advised us that we were approaching a "moment of truth." If the CEO (me) decided, and the board approved, the remaining members of the senior executive team had their choice: They could decide to support the new direction with enthusiasm; they could decide to continue to disagree (quietly) but still commit to supporting the new direction; or they could leave. As a result, three (roughly 30 percent) left. Today, as we look back, all who stayed were, over time, happy that we made the changes.

4. Debrief

The last phase, "debrief," may occur months or sometimes even years later. This is the time to review and determine whether or not the decision achieved its goals, and to evaluate what you did well, what you could have done better, and whether or not to continue. This is the time for the people who were against the decision originally to test whether their intuition was right, and—if so—to argue against continuing or repeating.

Sounds easy, doesn't it? It's not. Many obstacles can exist.

Obstacles

The most basic obstacle involves the spectrum of human behavior that I discussed earlier. If you have passive-aggressive or obnoxiously assertive people on your team, you have a problem.

Passive-aggressive people are useless in the discussion phase. They always agree, regardless of what they actually think. They're equally useless in the execution (delivery) phase because they often undermine it. The worst part is that you don't even know they disagree because they do their best to hide it. Passive-aggressive people can hide for years without discovery. You *must* find them and call them to task. If you have passive-aggressive people reporting to you who really can't change, you will need to ask them to leave.

At the other end of the spectrum, obnoxiously assertive people are easy to spot, but hard to work with. They're particularly difficult in the discussion phase because they inhibit meaningful dialogue. Most people either clam up in their presence or get so worked up emotionally that they can't contribute effectively. Again, I underscore the importance of surrounding yourself with people who can work with others on an adult-to-adult basis.

Lack of trust among teammates is another hindrance to effective decision-making. Without trust, people stop sharing their thoughts. Many factors can cause a lack of trust, but the most common is a lack of vulnerability. If someone (or, worse, multiple people) on your team refuses to be vulnerable, a lack of trust and ultimately a lack of communication will follow.

Vulnerability in this context means letting other people see who you are. Lack of vulnerability is equivalent to posing. People pose for many reasons. Some have something to hide. For example, a man who once reported to me wanted to hide something in his past. He was very protective of himself and his past, for understandable reasons. We could all sense it, yet none of us knew why at the time. All we knew for sure was that he was *hiding something*. Just knowing that caused us to lose trust.

Another of my direct reports had grown up with very demanding parents. If he didn't live up to his parents' expectations, they grew furious. One of the most common ways of falling short in his parents' eyes was being wrong, so he developed an irrational fear of it. To compensate, he was determined to always be right, and he put forth an exaggeratedly confident front implying that he was always right. He was obviously posing. Others sensed it and lost trust.

Another common example in organizations is people not understanding the rules of engagement. For example, a management team may have an agenda according to which they've all implicitly agreed to discuss a given problem on Friday, come to a solution, and commit to it. They may also have agreed that it's fine (perhaps even highly desirable) to prepare for Friday's discussion by talking about the problem in pairs or smaller groups in advance. So two team members, Tom and Jim, discuss it on Monday and agree on most aspects of the question. On Tuesday, Tom talks with Mary; Mary presents thoughts that are new to Tom, which makes him change his mind. But he doesn't go back and tell Jim that he's changed his mind since their discussion. Friday comes, and Jim is appalled that Tom seems committed to a different view than he expressed on Monday. Jim wonders if he can trust Tom.

Lack of trust is infectious and debilitating. It can bring down a whole team. Just one or two people posing can render an entire team dysfunctional. If you sense this is happening, you must trace it to its source and rout it out. Otherwise, it will hold you back, to your detriment, and ultimately to the detriment of your constituencies.

Other obstacles to following the Four Ds tend to be more team-specific than universal. For instance, at SVB we had a few additional hurdles that were an outgrowth of our past and seemed unique to our organization (although they might exist elsewhere). For example, my predecessor emphasized *consensus and harmony* to the extent that he actively discouraged disagreement or debate in meetings. Conflict went underground, which made it hard to get anything done since everyone felt entitled to object, even *after* the decision (*any* decision) had been made. Of course, these disagreements all took place in hallways, never in meetings. In the end, our consensus and our harmony were illusions. Everybody was posing.

When I was at SVB, I found that a number of people in middle management hesitated to state their opinions in discussions. Somehow, they believed it was not nice to disagree. Under my predecessor, it wasn't. When people disagreed in meetings, they were told to "take it off-line." These people became passive-aggressive, and their passive-aggressiveness surfaced during the delivery phase. People didn't want to cooperate in executing a decision they didn't fully agree with. They tended to think we were being heavy-handed or authoritarian when we insisted (and we did insist). Or they believed they'd been short-changed and should have been consulted. Actually, they *were* consulted. They were just too concerned about being "nice" to state their disagreement. Or, they felt that if they stated a different opinion, that others *had* to agree. Otherwise, they felt insulted.

Not knowing when to apply the Four Ds and when to do something else instead is the last obstacle I'll discuss. We constantly encounter situations requiring decisions. But we can't apply the Four Ds to them all. If we do, we "lock up" the organization in a kind of decision-making hell.

We have to be able to differentiate. Some questions are so big and important that we *must* apply the Four Ds. Some are so small that we should *never* apply the Four Ds; we should just decide on our own. Finally, we should delegate *many, if not most,* decisions to the next layer down. The people at that level, in turn, must be able to figure out if they should: 1) apply the Four Ds, 2) decide on their own, or 3) further delegate. And so it goes.

Many managers feel reluctant to delegate. Often, they're control freaks. Sometimes they're anxious people trying to make the best possible impression on their boss, so they want to "make sure" the job gets done right. In their view, the only way to achieve that is to do it themselves. This is a serious error on their part. They potentially deny themselves a better decision that they could have had if they'd consulted with others. In any case, they're denying their direct reports the learning experience of exercising judgment. Employees and team members who lack the chance to exercise judgment will not learn and therefore will not grow, and their job satisfaction will diminish. If they're good, they'll leave for greener pastures. If they're not good, they will likely stay, filling the organization with subpar team members.

WHO DECIDES WHAT

When using the Four Ds process, remember to clarify who decides and what's being decided. If the decider reports to you, you must give that person latitude to make the decision within parameters that you set. Then, you must monitor the quality of their decision-making over time. As you audit the outcome, step in to coach as needed. This is difficult in any case and especially when your direct report operates at a distance. If that person works overseas, for instance, you can't know or appreciate (as they do) the reality they're dealing with. It's not uncommon for leaders whose lieutenants are far away to grow less comfortable with delegating and lean more toward deciding things themselves. Sadly, this is the opposite of what would be most effective. In all cases, decisions should be made *as close to the ultimate client as possible.*

If you're working with people in distant locations, it's a huge mistake to take authority away from them because they're the only people who really understand what's going on in that region. Your decisions can't be as good as theirs because you won't understand the environment in the way that they do. They'll become discouraged and will lose the respect they're trying to garner from the people around them. It's a terrible thing to do, and unfortunately, it happens pretty often. Most American companies do this. Headquarters always thinks it knows better.

Finally, after your team makes a decision, as appropriate, you (or they) need to communicate it to the rest of the organization. It amazes me how often we forget to do that. We're so pleased about reaching a conclusion that we forget to tell everyone else. Unless you communicate your decisions, they probably won't be too useful.

Important Side Note

The Four Ds is all about consultative decision-making. It represents the heart of this field manual. The essence of consultative decision-making is this: When you make big decisions, there are at least four major possible approaches: democracy, consensus, dictatorship, and the Four Ds. Democracy is a failure to lead. Anybody can count votes; you don't need a leader to do that. Consensus is elusive, if not nonexistent. You could wait forever for consensus. Dictatorship is foolish. Those who make decisions without input from stakeholders and experts make poor decisions and seldom enjoy genuine support from the people they lead.

The approach practiced by the best leaders in history is the Four Ds (diversity in counsel, unity in action). The best leaders get input from stakeholders and experts first, and then (and only then) make decisions. Much of the time, the majority of the experts and stakeholders hold views that are consistent with the ultimate decision. But, *sometimes they don't.*

At times, as a leader, you will have to make decisions that are supported by neither the experts nor the stakeholders. In other words, there will be times when you will have to stand alone. You will have only yourself to fall back on. You will have to rely on your intestinal fortitude. That is leadership. If you are not capable of this, you cannot lead.

Ask yourself:

→ To what extent does our organization understand and appreciate the value of collaboration?

→ What has our organization done to create intelligent, culturally diverse, and professionally diverse teams?

→ To what extent do team members trust one another and show vulnerability?

→ What process(es) do we use for decision-making, for both day-to-day and big decisions?

→ What could we do to make better decisions (e.g., who's involved in the process, who takes responsibility for the decision, how is the decision executed, and how are processes and outcomes reviewed to learn what we might have done differently)?

CONFLICT ON YOUR TEAM

Conflict is a natural part of working together. It's the essence of collaborating with others; without conflict, nothing is accomplished. If we knew we were in agreement before a meeting, we wouldn't need to meet. But conflict can turn from being productive to destructive when: 1) it can't be resolved; or 2) it moves from issues to people, from ideas to personalities. As a leader, your job is to ensure that conflict gets resolved (but not necessarily to resolve it yourself).

This is not always easy. Sometimes two or more parties won't be able to resolve an issue. If it's a big enough issue, it may be necessary for *you* to un-delegate the power to decide and thus resolve it *yourself.* Reserve this approach for issues that: 1) affect the entire organization, 2) involve strategy, or 3) involve huge capital outlays or dents to the profit and loss.

If the issues don't fit into any of these three categories, you should encourage (and sometimes require) the warring parties to work it out between themselves. I recommend the following general procedure:

1. Assume the best of intentions on both sides. If you don't, the warring parties won't either.

2. Ask them to solve it on their own. You might coach either or both on how to approach the other. Try to get each to see the other's point of view. Encourage each person to spend more time trying to understand the other party and less time trying to make sure that the other party understands him/her.

3. If the warring parties are unsuccessful at resolving things, ask them to enlist a third, *neutral* party to help. At least initially, that third party should not be you.

4. If all else fails, you have only a few remaining options. You can play the third-party role yourself. You can decide for them, but in doing so you're setting a bad precedent. In a business, if necessary, you can fire one or both of them.

5. Good luck. If they can't resolve their differences, you may be better off without them.

MANAGING CONFLICT:
How to Disagree Without Getting Personal

Managing conflict between team members becomes more difficult when people take things personally, as they so often do.

Here's an example: After years of not getting along, Bill and Beth finally reached the point where they couldn't stand each other. Bill couldn't say enough bad things about Beth, and Beth felt the same way about him. The conflict became very personal. It had started gradually enough, as most animosities do. Bill talked too much for Beth's tastes. Whenever he took the floor in our management meetings, he seemed to ramble on forever. His vocabulary was large, and his mind moved quickly from concept to concept, from argument to argument. Keeping up with him was like trying to keep pace with a computer. Beth, judgmental and condescending, had a way of responding to Bill that looked and felt like a putdown. Bill was sensitive and came close to crying. Beth considered him irritating and weak. This scenario repeated itself week after week, to everyone's discomfort.

Interestingly, their respective interpretations of their interactions were anything but identical. Their ways of dealing with this conflict also differed. Beth felt she was guiltless. In her mind, she did nothing to provoke Bill; he was an annoyance and had to go. The problem was all his, and discussing it with him was useless. Bill saw things differently. Why was Beth so condescending to him? he often wondered aloud. What had he ever done to her?

Why wouldn't she just talk it over with him? What had he done to deserve this?

In my experience, most people are either more like Beth or more like Bill. For those like Beth, conflict brings out their inner sadist who insists that the other person is at fault; certainly, they could do no wrong. (Might this stance stem from such deep insecurity that they morbidly fear the possibility of actually being wrong?) Or, for those like Bill, conflict brings out their inner masochist who fears that it's all their fault, but still can't help wondering why everyone always picks on them (the martyr complex).

Neither type realizes that it's almost impossible to know exactly what another person thinks, or why he or she thinks it. Why? Everyone carries the baggage of their entire past experience, which influences them deeply although they're largely unaware of it. We all perceive the world through a filter strongly colored by past experiences, and the way we respond to things is also heavily influenced by those past experiences. In neither case do we realize how much we're influenced by the past.

Perhaps Bill's parents always condescended to him. When Beth acts a certain way, in light of his past, Bill perceives her actions as condescending. He responds to that perception in ways informed by his past. Perhaps his parents always insisted that they were right, and Bill was wrong. That might lead Bill to always respond defensively to Beth as if he actually was wrong. ("Why does she treat me this way? What have I done to deserve it? Why can't we just talk it over?")

We could imagine a similar, albeit different, set of circumstances to explain Beth's behavior.

Graphically, almost any communication between two people looks like this:

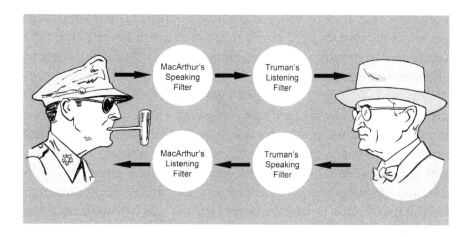

(As a historical example, communications between President Harry Truman and General Douglas MacArthur, whose first meeting on Wake Island was famously marred by this type of dynamic, worsened over time until Truman finally got fed up and fired MacArthur.)[35]

Bill will never really know what Beth thinks or feels, or why she acts as she does. Neither will Beth ever truly understand Bill's thoughts, feelings, or actions. We're all heavily influenced, in our perceptions, thoughts, feelings, and responses, by our past experiences. No one ever really knows what other people's past experiences looked like. Most of the time, we're not even too clear on our own.

What can we learn from this? First, it's almost useless for Bill to spend time wondering why Beth treats him this way. It mostly has little to do with Bill, and much to do with Beth. Or vice versa. Second, the best we can do is to try to recognize cause-and-effect relationships. Bill might notice: "Whenever I talk too long, too fast, and with too much complexity, Beth responds with what

---

35 H.W. Brands, *The General vs. the President: MacArthur and Truman at the Brink of Nuclear War* (New York: Anchor Books, 2017), 172–189.

looks to me like condescension." He might then reflect: "This has more to do with Beth than with me, but if I want her to treat me differently, I will need to act differently. Let me try not talking too long, too fast, and in too complicated a way, and see what happens." Beth, for her part, could undertake a similar exercise. One fundamental truth: we cannot change others' behavior; we can change only our own.

An organization as a whole can get into a funk if too many people are in conflict *that they take personally.* This is almost always a result of the leader. If a leader takes conflict personally or does not know how to coach others who take conflict personally, the organization as a whole will suffer. The good news? As a leader, you're in a unique position to solve this problem and make the organization well again. A positive, collaborative attitude and culture start at the top with you.

Remember, leading a team takes tremendous work in the best of times. In challenging times, it may feel like it's taking everything you've got. But your hard work is worth the effort. Your organization will be much stronger if you have a diverse team and *still stand together.*

THE IMPORTANCE OF MEETINGS

Meetings are the lifeblood of organizations, and yet, American culture seems to eschew meetings. This notion is misguided. A meeting is simply a face-to-face communication. Communication is absolutely necessary, and face-to-face is often more effective than digital. True, many meetings are useless—but that's because people don't always know how to make them effective, not because meetings (communications) are inherently a waste of time. Many people believe that famed football coach Knute Rockne once said, "Most men, when they think they are thinking, are merely rearranging their prejudices." That sure sounds like some ineffective meetings that I've been in—how about you? Take the time to meet with your team members, creating a space where they feel comfortable contributing and are interested in really listening to each other. If you don't, you and your team are missing a valuable opportunity to engage in new ideas and better ways of doing things.

I know many managers who rarely meet with their direct reports one-on-one. In my opinion, these managers are failing to fulfill their responsibility. I recommend at least one scheduled full-hour meeting per month, one-on-one, with each direct report, and as many shorter meetings in between as appropriate and necessary.

TYPES OF MEETINGS AND TYPICAL PROBLEMS[36]

If you haven't noticed already, your life has become a series of back-to-back meetings. A day full of ineffective meetings takes its toll on productivity.

It's the leader's job to:

1. Create a culture.

2. Build, lead, and coach the management team.

3. Get everyone pointed in the right direction.

4. Make some very big decisions, and create a framework within which others can make many other decisions.

5. Resolve differences.

6. Ensure the creation of processes that enable others to execute effectively.

7. Communicate effectively with all constituencies.

---

36 For an in-depth description of all of the various types of meetings and their many pitfalls, see Patrick Lencioni, *Death by Meeting: A Leadership Fable* (San Francisco: Wiley, 2004).

These activities don't happen in a vacuum. They involve others, so effective meetings are crucial.

To start, you'll want to be clear on what kind of meeting you're holding:

Update Meetings

"Update" meetings are shorter and more frequent than most other types. Typically, your team just updates each other on things that have happened or that would be of interest to the others. At SVB, my eight-person team held update meetings at least weekly. I recommend meeting at a round table. The advantage: Everyone can see each other's faces, which is important, and oblong tables often don't allow for that. We had one team member who would always "zone out" if we were sitting around an oblong table. So, I resolved: always a round table. Just go around the table, with everyone taking five to ten minutes to say what they've been up to. Questions are allowed, but if questions devolve into discussions, note the need for a discussion, resolve to postpone until the next "discussion" meeting (as opposed to update meeting), and move on.

Discussion (Decision-making) Meetings

I recommend holding discussion meetings less frequently. You can attach them to the report-only meetings, but be careful not to run them together. In discussion meetings, the table shape and participant number is even more important. It's *critical* that everyone can see each other's faces (so use a round table) and that no more than eight people attend. Studies show that seven or eight is the maximum number of people who can participate in a discussion before posturing and politics set in.

Unlike report-only meetings, decision-making meetings are very complex and require serious preparation by participants and the leader.

The more time you spend preparing for decision-making meetings, the better. Before the meeting, decide what kinds of topics you're willing to discuss. It's a little like being in charge of the Supreme Court. You get to decide which "cases" you'll hear. In making that decision, you're simultaneously deciding which cases others farther down in the organization will hear. In other words, the more decisions you make at the top, the fewer decisions people farther down in the organization will have a chance to make. And vice versa. In the end, there's an optimal proportion at either end of the spectrum. You want to make enough decisions at the top to provide adequate direction to the rest of the organization. Yet you want people at the lower levels to make enough decisions that they'll have latitude to exercise judgment, feel motivated, and have enough jurisdiction over tactics so they can do their jobs without stumbling over you. Generally, you should only hear cases that involve culture, strategy, organizationally significant outlays of capital or subtractions from the profit and loss, or similar items that impact the entire organization, or at least large parts of it.

The meeting leader determines *the content and length of the agenda*. There's an art to this. Ensure enough time to cover necessary topics and plan to discuss few enough topics so your people have the energy to handle them. Only you can decide how much time is enough. Don't cut short a discussion that needs to be longer. And only you can decide whether your team has enough energy to go on to the next topic. Don't push them beyond that point or you won't do justice to either the topic or the group.

Like you, your people must prepare. Presenters should provide advance materials to the group to give people a chance to think beforehand and avoid wasting time in the group setting acquainting others with background material. We had our meetings on Mondays and required each discussion leader to send the group background materials by the end of Friday so people could peruse them over the weekend.

Background materials must be self-explanatory. They need to:

1. Describe the issue (what is being discussed and why),

2. Provide the organizational background and context (why and to whom this issue is important),

3. Clarify the question (what needs to be answered),

4. Outline the options (what possible answers exist),

5. Recommend (which option does the discussion leader prefer?), and

6. Describe exactly what the discussion leader wants to leave the meeting with (approval for a particular recommendation, feedback on the decision, group consensus, etc.).

America has grown used to PowerPoint. There's nothing inherently wrong with PowerPoint any more than there's anything wrong with Word documents. Both applications are useful in different scenarios. However, people tend to associate Word with complete sentences and PowerPoint with "pidgin English"—which works just fine if there's a presenter to translate. If not, it's often hard to know who's doing what to whom. Since background materials are read in isolation before a meeting, they must be self-explanatory, so writers should use complete sentences.

Other Types of Meetings

"Business reviews" and "big picture" discussions are also constructive. In business reviews, you ask each business unit or support group to present their numbers, explaining why they are what they are. Everyone's allowed to ask questions and make suggestions.

"Big picture" discussions cover a general topic to find out what each team member thinks. The desired outcome? Simply that team members understand each other better, not that they achieve consensus. Personally, I like holding big-picture meetings over dinner. A topic might be: "What attributes do we value most in employment candidates, and how do we interview to identify the presence of these attributes?"

Through these types of meetings, you and your team can learn a lot about each other and how to do things better.

Finally, from time to time, you'll want to have strategic meetings. You might discuss things like entering new lines of business or new geographies, or acquiring companies of a different profile, all within the context of the existing strategy. Occasionally, you might even question the strategy itself to see if it needs modification. Strategic meetings typically occur off-site, are at least one or two days long, and need much preparation to be productive.

LEADING THE MEETING

If you're the group leader, you'll need to spend some additional time—after reading background materials, but before the meeting—to make sure you know: 1) exactly what the question is (i.e., how to frame it most productively), and 2) what techniques you might employ to move the discussion to a productive conclusion.

Ground Rules

If you haven't already, make sure everybody (including yourself) is clear on the ground rules. No matter how experienced your team members are at discussion, no matter how direct they're used to being with each other, and no matter how long they've worked together effectively, ground rules are crucial. I recommend the following:

1. Stick to the issues. Avoid talking about people.

2. Be more interested in learning what others think and why than in telling others what *you* think and why.

3. View the outcome as being like a sculpture that you're all trying to shape. Discussion should not be "mortal combat"; it should be "group-inspired discovery."

4. Make sure everyone is heard (even those who are less assertive). The quiet ones may be as smart, or perhaps even smarter, than the assertive ones.

5. Never, *ever* contribute to someone feeling stupid.

6. On the other hand, all team members must try to be thick-skinned enough to accept when others respectfully disagree with them.

7. If the group (or individuals within the group) needs more time to think or caucus, postpone the conclusion, perhaps to a subsequent meeting.

8. As a leader, you should hold back until others have spoken. Otherwise, you run the risk of inadvertently discouraging people from expressing the very thoughts you need to hear in order to make the best decision in the end.

9. Until the decision has been made, encourage opposing views. Afterward, don't.

Framing the Issue and Expected Outcome

As a group leader, another responsibility is framing the issue and being clear about the discussion's goal. How the question is framed can determine whether it can be answered, how long (and with how much wear and tear on the team) it will take to answer, and whether the answer will be useful and actionable. As a leader, you have an obligation to the group to ensure that the question is properly framed. You don't have to figure out the proper framing yourself. Other team members can help you. But it's your responsibility to make sure the question is properly framed.

Before starting, you must also make clear to your team the expected outcome of the discussion. Why is your group having this discussion? This bears repeating because: 1) lack of clarity about the discussion's goal is a frequent cause of team discontent, and 2) I myself have the most trouble remembering to do this.

Once your question is properly framed, you must tell your team—before starting the discussion—which of the following is the discussion's goal:

1. I've already made a decision, this is what it is, and I want your advice on implementing it.

2. I've already made a decision, but I want your opinion on whether or not it is a good one.

3. I have a decision to make, and I want your input.

4. I have a decision to make, I want to discuss it with you, and then I want you to vote on it.

5. We have a decision to make, I'd like you to discuss it (perhaps even without me there), and I'd like you to decide and then let me know the outcome.

TECHNIQUES FOR PRODUCTIVE MEETINGS

You've framed the question and clarified your discussion goal. Now you can start talking. Whatever your style, you may wish to apply the following techniques to facilitate and optimize the discussion. I'm sure you'll discover more useful techniques on your own over time.

1. **Write it down.** As people share opinions or make points, write them on large sheets of paper taped to the walls or displayed on easels. Do not attach names to opinions. This will depersonalize the discussion (making people focus on ideas rather than who thought of them) and help people remember what's been said.

2. **Engage everyone.** Some people are more expressive than others. If two or three people do most of the talking, ask the quieter ones what they're thinking.

3. **Encourage clarification.** As a leader, hold back but encourage others to clarify their thoughts: "Rachel, can you help us understand what you mean by that?" or "Mary, help us understand why you believe that to be the case?"

4. **Break down into smaller groups of two and three for a few minutes.** When you're caught in a logjam, divide into small groups, and have the groups go "off-line" for about twenty minutes and then come back to the main group to report on their discussion. Sometimes you may wish to divide an issue into two or three questions and have each small group pursue a different one. Or one small group could discuss the pros and the other the cons. Alternatively, divide into task forces and adjourn; continue later.

5. **Pros and cons.** Use the "Ben Franklin ledger." Draw an empty balance sheet and ask the group to help you put all of the cons on one side and the pros on the other. Or set up another empty balance sheet, this time asking the group to help you put areas of general agreement on one side and areas of general disagreement on the other.

6. **Love it?** Go around the room, asking people to state their level of agreement (love it, like it, think it's okay, don't like it but can live with it, can't live with it).

7. **And why?** Again, go around the table, asking each person to give a two-minute impromptu speech on where they stand on the issue, and why.

8. **Take a nonbinding vote.** List the options and vote. A variant, if there are several options: Each person has two (or three) votes, but they can give only one vote to any single item.

How long should the discussion last? There's no single answer. In fact, there are likely as many answers as there are people in the room. Each person will have a feeling for how much discussion time is enough. Only you can decide, though, and you'll have to live with the fact that nobody else will agree with you. As a leader, it's your responsibility to decide. How well you decide will be a function of: 1) your understanding of the issue; 2) your understanding of the motivations, beliefs, feelings, and agendas of the individuals in the room; and 3) your courage.

At the end of the discussion, you'll need to do the following:

1. Clarify what's been accomplished through the discussion.

2. Clarify the next step(s).

3. Clarify who's responsible for making them.

Ask yourself:

→ How do we prepare for and conduct meetings in our organization, and how effective are they?

→ What ground rules do we observe in our meetings?

→ How effective am I at framing issues and articulating expected outcomes for our meetings?

→ How effective are my team members and I in facilitating and optimizing discussion in our meetings?

→ How could we do better?

CHAPTER 6

COMMUNICATING WITH YOUR CONSTITUENCIES

Keeping Everyone in the Loop

This chapter is about how to communicate effectively with your direct reports, with all of the people in your organization as a whole, and with any outside constituencies. It presents a number of time-honored principles, which—if you follow them—will guarantee that your communications are effective.

"It was a nation . . . that had the lion heart.
I had the luck to be called upon to give the roar." [37]

WINSTON CHURCHILL

As a leader, your primary job—beyond building and coaching a team and creating a culture—is communicating: with your team, your employees, and your outside constituencies (including clients,

---

37 Winston Churchill, "Wonderful Honor," in Richard Toye, *The Roar of the Lion: The Untold Story of Churchill's World War II Speeches*, (Oxford: Oxford University Press, 2013), 1.

board, investors, regulators, government entities, and your community). Your main topic? It's always the same and yet always exciting: where your organization has come from, where it is today, and where it's headed. In essence, your job is communicating the story of your organization, culminating in your *vision* of its glorious future.

For many people in positions of leadership, this sounds difficult. Many aspiring leaders seem to dread the mandate of communication. Some find it intimidating. They remember how much they hated giving speeches in front of large audiences. Others find it boring. They wonder why they need to keep telling people the same things over and over. Remember, some of history's greatest orators faced the same or similar challenges and worked hard to overcome them and to perfect the skills that brought them fame. British Prime Minister Winston Churchill, for instance, who rallied the nation during World War II, practiced enunciation in his youth to correct a lisp. He labored over his communications and chose different rhetorical methods, like using short, familiar words and ending speeches with a "rapid succession of waves of sound and vivid pictures." Churchill, who wrote his own speeches, said that he spent an hour working on every minute of a speech he made. He knew the importance of frequent communication and used his weekly radio address to inspire people around the world. "In the dark days and darker nights when England stood alone," said John F. Kennedy, "and most men save Englishmen despaired of England's life—he mobilized the English language and sent it into battle."[38]

Finally, many leaders who aren't comfortable communicating fall back on the adage that "actions speak louder than words." Sadly, good actions alone are not enough. It is just as important to tell people what you've done as it is to do it. Actions without words are like sending roses without a card.

---

38 Tom Vitale, "Winston Churchill's Way with Words," *Weekend Edition Saturday*, National Public Radio, July 14, 2012, accessed April 9, 2018, https://www.npr.org/2012/07/14/156720829/winston-churchills-way-with-words.

THE IMPORTANCE OF OVER-COMMUNICATING

"Over-communicating" sounds like an unnecessary action. In fact, there's a useful place for it. Let's examine where it's actually helpful. Over-communication that makes listeners feel that you don't trust them and don't think they'll come through is obviously not productive. For example, asking your spouse if she took out the garbage for the third time sounds like nagging and will certainly give her the feeling that you don't trust her to actually follow through. But it *is* appropriate for information with a liturgical value, like repetitive lines in a sermon or speech that rekindle the listeners' sense of belonging. Winston Churchill, for example, effectively used repetition in his 1940 speech to the House of Commons as he described the possibility of Germany invading Britain. By repeating "we shall fight," he strengthened his message of future victory to the British people, helping them envision what was coming and how by banding together they would prevail:

> We shall go on to the end, we shall fight in France, we shall fight on the seas and oceans, we shall fight with growing confidence and growing strength in the air, we shall defend our Island, whatever the cost may be, we shall fight on the beaches, we shall fight on the landing grounds, we shall fight in the fields and in the streets, we shall fight in the hills; we shall never surrender . . .[39]

Just as selective repetition, or over-communication, can strengthen a speech, you can also use it in your daily life as a leader. Some things are important to repeat. As CEO, for example, I would often remind my team of our purpose, our values, and our current set of three or four company-wide goals. I repeated this message, not because I thought my team had forgotten or wouldn't reach the goals, but to

---

39 Winston Churchill, "We Shall Fight on the Beaches," June 4, 1940, House of Commons (speech), International Churchill Society website, accessed June 3, 2021, https://winstonchurchill.org/resources/speeches/1940-the-finest-hour/we-shall-fight-on-the-beaches/.

solidify the feeling that we were all in this together, we all belonged together, and we would all achieve success together.

Unfortunately, most managers misuse repetition. They over-communicate on tasks they want to be done and under-communicate on the liturgical types of speech that inspire others. Or, they make important decisions, yet fail to announce them. A decision that no one knows about is often as good as no decision at all. Reminding people over and over of tasks you have assigned will cause them to believe you don't trust them, and they will lose interest in completing them.

Finally, I want to mention something that I experienced with one of my direct reports who is my polar opposite (I'm fairly extroverted, she's extremely introverted). This manager never seemed interested in other people's opinions because she believed it was her job—and hers alone—to solve problems. One of her direct reports told me, "I feel lonely in her presence." My management style, by contrast, is that I think by talking with others. I spend my whole day talking. I'll walk into an office, for example, and say that I'm having a problem with something and start drawing on the whiteboard. So I'm thinking things through by expressing myself, and the person I'm working with is feeling valued because he/she is on the front lines with me. The opposite, which results from a leader never asking others' opinions, is a direct report who thinks: "I don't feel the leader trusts me. He/she is not asking my opinion and insists on deciding things without my input." Your direct reports won't feel valued if you never ask for their thoughts and ideas. And you'll be limited to your narrow range of experience. If you're the kind of person who can't comfortably talk with and deal with people and be genuinely interested in their ideas and opinions—or perhaps you just don't want to—then why would you want to be a CEO or a leader? Is it just for recognition? If you are congenitally constrained in this way, why would you yearn to go into a profession or role that revolves around just that? Let someone else be the CEO or leader and go into another profession that doesn't require those skills. That just doesn't make sense to me.

*"You cannot lead a battle if you think
you look silly on a horse."*[40]

NAPOLEON BONAPARTE

COMMUNICATING WITH YOUR TEAM

First, your direct reports: it's important to communicate with them as a group, *and just as important,* individually. Visit informally with each of your direct reports at least once a week, and at least monthly on a formal (meaning *scheduled*) basis. Frequent communication: 1) helps your team members understand the culture you're cultivating, your vision, and your priorities; and 2) helps you understand what challenges your team members are facing so you can offer coaching on how to overcome the obstacles. It's *not* to tell them what to do, and even less to tell them how to do it. If you have to tell your team members what to do (and how to do it), you have the wrong people reporting to you and need to fix that problem first. If you have the right people reporting to you, telling them what to do and how to do it will most certainly rob them of their motivation.

As a leader, what you choose to talk about will have great symbolic value. Don't waste your time on unimportant topics, unless, of course, they fit into the category of relationship-building. In that case, the conversation topics may be inherently trivial, but they're important because they strengthen your relationship.

Incidentally, if you don't ask your direct reports about the challenges they're facing, and if you fail to offer suggestions (*not* commands) on how best to deal with those problems, your team will think their challenges aren't important to you, and you'll be seen as uncaring and unsupportive. Your team needs to know what you think is important regarding culture, vision, and priorities. And you need to

40 Attributed to Napoleon Bonaparte, AZQuotes.com, accessed October 14, 2018,
https://www.azquotes.com/quote/1059330.

know what's important to your team—particularly their challenges—and offer suggestions as appropriate. On the other hand, your suggestions should be just that—*suggestions*, not orders. Otherwise, your direct reports will never learn to think for themselves.

Do *not* contribute to "triangulation." It's human nature to talk about other people behind their backs, but don't do it. And don't allow others to do it, either, unless it's constructive. It's fine for you to say, or listen to a direct report say, something positive about another of your direct reports in that person's absence. But it's not okay for you to say, or listen to another direct report say, something negative. Discipline yourself not to indulge in this behavior, and discourage others from doing so. If a direct report says something bad about another of your direct reports in your presence when that other person is absent, strongly encourage him/her to directly address the issue with the person in question. If he/she needs help on *how* to do this, it's fine for you to offer coaching. But do not indulge that person's desire to negatively discuss a third person (who also reports to you) behind his/her back.

I understand that talking directly to people about problems you have with them can be difficult. That notwithstanding, if Jim says something bad to you about Jane, you might say, "I think you need to talk to Jane about it, not to me." Later, check in with Jim: "Did you talk to Jane?" Even if Jim says yes, check in with Jane and ask her if Jim discussed the issue with her. Likely, Jane will say no, that she never heard anything about it. Often, this is because people (in this case, Jim) tend to report their interactions with others in ways that make them sound more explicit than they actually were. They might portray themselves as being incredibly direct when in actuality they just hinted at the subject in a way that the other person didn't even pick up on.

When two people talk, they hear what's coming at them through a filter informed by all their past experiences. Rarely does the other person receive your words exactly as you meant them. You may say something you think is innocuous, but to the other person, it sounds inflammatory. You never know what the other person thinks you said. And the other person never hears quite what you meant to say. So make an effort to be as clear as possible, and keep this in mind when you're helping others to navigate the choppy waters of communication.

At SVB, we used the "9th Guiding Principle," which basically says: "Do not talk negatively about others behind their backs, and don't allow others to do so, either."

Follow this principle alone, and you'll go a long way toward discouraging politics in your organization.

Encourage teamwork instead of internal competition (except the most harmless, fun sort) while following the 9th Guiding Principle, and you'll go a long way toward helping to eliminate politics.

Follow both suggestions (the 9th Guiding Principle and encouraging teamwork/discouraging internal competition), *and* fire anyone who doesn't follow these two suggestions, and you may actually eradicate politics altogether.

COMMUNICATING WITH YOUR EMPLOYEES

Your employees and team members expect to have a relationship with you. They're members of your tribe and expect to know their chief. Their happiness depends in some considerable measure on their perception of you. So you need to be visible *and* audible. Most will never "know" you, at least not to the extent that your friends and relatives do, but if they never see or hear from you, they'll feel that they don't know you at all.

Walk around. Show up at events. Hold town meetings. Know as many of their names as possible. Look people in the eye. Address them by name, if you can. Even if you can't, address them. Be friendly, bold, and open.

As CEO, I stayed in regular contact with our (at that time) one thousand-plus employees, using various means to do so. Periodically,

I'd send a short email to them all, usually congratulating them for some corporate success. Often, on our one thousand-plus person Monday-morning conference call (yes, all one thousand-plus of us, every Monday morning at 8:15), I'd address them. When something really important happened, I'd hold a special conference call on Tuesday or Wednesday morning, at which I was often (although not always) the only speaker, to talk to them directly. From time to time, along with other members of my team (we focused on being a confidence-inspiring management team, rather than on having a single charismatic leader), I'd appear on our intranet portal via streaming video. Several times a year, I held town meetings with sixty or seventy of our employees in the auditorium that I built explicitly for that purpose. Once a year, I'd go on my "tour," ensuring that I was in front of each and every employee worldwide (in groups of fifty to one hundred) to talk about who we were, where we'd come from, where we were currently, and where we were headed in the coming year.

I always made a point of speaking openly and honestly. If they posed a question I couldn't answer for a good reason (i.e., answering would constitute a violation of Regulation FD), I told them so and, of course, didn't answer it. But to the extent I could, I told them everything, honestly and openly.

And, something that many leaders find difficult, I would often talk with them about my personal life: I'd mention my wife, my children, my dog, my brothers. Doing so made our employees feel that I was open and down-to-earth. Doing so made me a real person for them.

As much as possible, smile and be cheerful. Your employees' view of the organization's health (*and therefore of their security*) depends on that. If you walk around frowning (or just walk around with a "closed brow" because you're thinking) people will interpret that as a sure sign that things aren't going well with the organization. To them, you *are* the organization. It would never occur to most of them that you might be unhappy about something that one of your teenagers had done, or anything else for that matter. In their minds, if you're frowning, it must have something to do with the organization and how bad it's doing. If they ask you how you're doing, you can be certain that they're really wondering (even if they aren't aware of it) how the organization is doing. If you're not smiling and being cheerful, the organization isn't doing well in their perception. And if the organization isn't doing well, their security is threatened.

Employees and team members have expectations of their top leaders. It's not enough to be cheerful. You also need to be fair, kind, confident, and dignified. If you fail to be any of these things, you undermine their confidence. If you don't want the burden of being all of these things, don't be the leader. You will need to be these things *really*, in real life. You can't just fake it and expect to get away with it. As a top-ranking leader, you must be authentic. If you're not, your employees and team members will notice it over time.

Finally, your employees, just like your significant other, expect you to be appreciative. If you're naturally incapable of showing appreciation, you shouldn't be in the top ranks. You'll need to express appreciation regularly to groups and individuals. As CEO, I often began my speeches by expressing genuine appreciation for our employees' hard work, and for the sacrifices they made in the service of our clients. I also made a point of knowing what good deeds others had done, and of expressing my appreciation for those specific good deeds. For example, every couple of months I sent out a request, via email, to the "top 100" (out of 1,000) employees, asking them to tell me about good things (specific things, not just generally good behavior patterns) that others had done. Then, on one of my many plane rides, I'd handwrite notes to each person who had done something good, stating exactly *what* they'd done (not just "for being a good employee"). Then we'd send out the notes with gifts (wine, candy, gift certificates). I can't tell you how many cubicles in our company had at least one of these cherished notes attached to their inside walls.

There are a thousand ways to show your appreciation. Pick a few that fit *you* and deploy them. Your employees will feel your recognition, and it will motivate them and help make them happy to be part of your organization.

Someone once said that as CEO, you need to have a "love affair" with each of your direct reports. Of course, this is not to be taken literally. But you do need to develop a personal relationship with each and every one of them. I remember one of my successors in a management position who had trouble with this. He felt that his job was deciding things and that he could earn his direct reports' respect by being an excellent "decider." He held one-on-ones, to be sure, but used them only to impart his decisions—not to build personal relationships. Over time, his direct reports felt alienated and mistrusted. Deep down, they were hoping he would ask their opinions, and even if he didn't adopt them, at least express appreciation and admiration for their ideas. Because he decided everything himself, they felt he didn't trust their ability. The best people left for greener pastures where they'd have room to grow. Sadly, by not soliciting their opinions, this manager denied himself the opportunity to benefit from their wisdom, and the quality of his decision-making suffered.

A note on remembering names:

How important is it to remember names? I have to admit, I might have answered this differently twenty years ago. I am lucky to have been born with an excellent short-term memory, and because remembering names was pretty easy for me, I would have said, yes, of course, you should try to remember the names of all of the people in your organization. Clearly, there is no sweeter sound for anyone than the sound of their own name. On the other hand, even excellent memories have their limits. When I began my tenure as CEO, we had only one thousand employees and I was determined to know all of them by name.

Accordingly, I asked our HR department to create a picture database of all of our employees. This, in and of itself, was difficult because many heads of HR, rightly or wrongly (I actually am not sure which), would interpret this request as a breach of privacy. Then, I had it printed for myself and took it with me on plane rides, during which I spent hours memorizing it. When I would arrive at one of our more than thirty-five offices around the world, I had each name and face combination firmly in mind (at least for that particular office). Generally, I'd hold an all-hands meeting with the employees and would amaze them by going around the room and referring to each of them by name. I think they were flattered, but I have to admit, I enjoyed amazing them. As time went by, that became more and more difficult. Then one day in Colorado, at an office with at that time about fifty employees, I made it through the first forty-nine and failed on the fiftieth. Later, I learned that I'd really hurt that one person's feelings and that the damage I'd done by failing at one was greater than the good I'd done by succeeding at the first forty-nine. Also, I had to admit that I was sort of showing off, which is never a good idea. After that, I stopped the practice.

COMMUNICATING WITH YOUR OTHER CONSTITUENCIES (CLIENTS, REGULATORS, GOVERNMENT ENTITIES, COMMUNITY, ETC.)

Stay in regular, constant contact with your outside constituencies. You need to know what they're thinking, about the experience they're having with your organization, and about their future given whatever is happening in their respective markets. You may have some form of institutionalized market research undertaken by either insiders or outsiders. That's important. But you also need to undertake some of your own, directly, to ensure that the only filter is your own.

The client companies I worked with were spread across the country. I traveled about 40 percent of the time to visit with our clients, either individually or in groups (usually seven to ten people over dinner). My purpose was always the same: to tell them our story (where we'd come from, where we were currently, and where we were going), to discover what they thought and felt about the experience they were having with us, and to learn how they viewed their future. I would use this information to augment whatever I learned through others, which in turn helped me chart our course effectively.

For the most part, this approach can be applied to all of your outside constituencies, not just clients. That said, I recommend getting specialist advice from relevant experts on dealing with the press.

Choose the Appropriate Style

Different audiences require different styles. If you communicate exactly the same message in exactly the same way to each of your constituencies, they'll each hear something different. That's a basic tenet of modern communications theory. Here's why: your constituencies all come from different places, and each applies a unique filter. To communicate successfully, change your style—and sometimes even the message itself—to fit your audience.

For example, if you were proposing marriage, you'd probably say something like: "I want to spend my life with you. I love you more than I've ever loved anyone. You're perfect for me. I like everything about you. We're perfectly matched, and we'll have a wonderful life together." At SVB, a lending business, when we wanted to close a deal, we'd say much the same: "We admire your company, and we believe you should be proud of what you've accomplished. You represent exactly the kind of company we want to do business with. We'd be proud to be your partner. We'll enjoy a wonderful relationship together, with us supporting you as you grow and prosper."

But the loan officer who just said that to the prospect would describe *the same situation* differently to the loan committee. It would sound more like: "This is a pretty good company. Management is honest and reasonably competent. We expect the company to succeed operationally, but even if it doesn't, we believe the company or at least our collateral can be sold for more than the value of our debt." If the loan officer said the same thing to the company that he said to the loan committee, he'd never close the deal.

Finally, you may want to treat all direct reports exactly the same, for the sake of fairness, but if you do, you'll be sub-optimizing your team and actually treating at least some of them unfairly. Why? Because some will need to talk with you daily; for others, that may be stifling. Some are at a developmental stage requiring plenty of support and attention; for others, this could feel smothering or perhaps even threatening.

Gauge your audience's needs and desires. If you don't, you won't be communicating what you mean to.

Avoid Surprises

Have you ever seen the old television show *Dear John*? It always started with the same scene: John, a middle-aged teacher, comes home from work to find the house empty and a "Dear John" note on the mantel. The premise: He had no warning. Why hadn't his wife told him before that she was unhappy? Well, there are at least two possibilities: 1) She *had* told him, at least subtly, and he just hadn't listened; or 2) there's a first time for everything.

People hate surprises. Invariably they ask, "Why didn't you tell me before?" Frankly, no matter how soon you share bad news, they'll always ask why you didn't tell them sooner. The best policy? Tell them as soon as you know, even if you're not yet certain. You'll never be able to tell them before you know, but if you can show that you at least warned them as soon as you suspected (and even before you actually knew), you'll remain on high ground, and they'll keep viewing you as a leader with integrity. If you take it upon yourself to decide for them "when they need to know," you'll invite their anger and mistrust.

Repeat Yourself, Often

People often don't hear something until you've said it so often *you're* sure you're driving them crazy by repeating. Studies show that the average audience member listens to a speaker only about 30 percent of the time. The rest of the time, he or she daydreams. This is true most of the time, in any type of meeting. What does this mean for the speaker? Repeat your messages several times to make sure everyone hears them. But express those messages differently each time, for two reasons: a) to avoid annoying those who were actually listening, and b) to address the needs of those who actually were listening but still didn't understand because *your initial way* of explaining was unclear to them.

Consider these lines from Winston Churchill's "Blood, Toil, Tears, and Sweat" speech. Which word does he repeat, in a series of varying sentences? What is the ultimate message that he wants to impart? "You ask, what is our aim? I can answer in one word: Victory. Victory at all costs. Victory in spite of all terror. Victory, however long and hard the road may be, for without victory there is no survival."[41]

Effective communication is difficult. Successful leaders limit the number of messages to various constituencies, but repeat them often, and frequently vary the way they express themselves.

Always Tell the Truth, the Whole Truth, and Nothing but the Truth

In my experience, people spend too much time on *spin*. Often, when something has gone wrong and leaders are uncomfortable talking about it, they devote time and energy to figuring out the best way to spin it to avoid upsetting their audience. The problem is, most people will recognize spin for what it is. Once that happens, they become skeptical. And when they become skeptical, the

---

41 Winston Churchill, "Blood, Toil, Tears and Sweat" (speech, House of Commons, London, England, May 13, 1940), *Never Give In!*, 206.

leader is burdened with a credibility deficit that may take a long time to eradicate. Far better, in my view, is to face the music, "call a spade a spade," and deal with the consequences. "Spinning," in my view, is bad in two ways. First of all, it borders on not telling the truth, which is in and of itself not good. And second, it often if not invariably leaves the speaker with the enduring burden of a credibility deficit.

Example: I remember a point in time, perhaps twenty years ago, when we began offering a new product. Like all commercial banking products, the product itself, as well as the way in which it was delivered, was governed by federal regulation. Through an audit, we learned that we had delivered this product in a way that was prohibited by a certain regulation. Now, to be specific, a case could be made that we had violated the *spirit* of the regulation, but not necessarily the *letter* of the regulation. Of course, this was a public matter because if the regulators felt that the spirit was more important than the letter, first of all, they were right, because regulators are—by definition—always right. And second of all, if the regulators were right, we would have to tell all of the clients who had purchased the product what we had done wrong and what we would do to fix it. Without my knowledge, our legal staff chose to defend the product, taking the view that we had *not* violated the *letter* of the regulation. Well, they were wrong, at least in my view. Taking this approach left us vis-à-vis the regulators with the burden of a credibility deficit, and because we then had to self-report to all the clients who had bought the product, vis-à-vis our clients as well. The entire legal staff knew the difference between the letter of the regulation and the spirit of the regulation. We would have been far better off if we'd just owned up to our mistake in the first place, done what was required, and put it behind us.

First Build Rapport, Then Deliver Your Message

When I worked in North Carolina forty years ago, I had a good boss and a good relationship with him. One day, he sat me down and told a long, seemingly irrelevant story. I wondered where on earth he was going with it. He talked about the neighborhood he grew up in, his parents, and their relationship with neighbors. Then he described a disagreement his parents once had with a neighbor and how his father successfully resolved it.

He said his father had kept his suit on one Sunday after church, instead of changing into something more casual, as was his custom. After Sunday dinner, still dressed in his suit, he visited the neighbor in question. They sat on the front porch and talked. The neighbor offered him iced tea, and they talked further. Hours went by. Just before standing up to go home for supper, my boss's father brought up the issue underlying the disagreement, almost as if in passing. They dealt with it quickly and amicably. When my boss finished telling me this story, he paused, and said: "I think you could learn something from the way my father approached things."

In other words, build rapport first, then communicate. If your constituencies like you, they'll be much more interested in hearing your views, which may (or may not) diverge from their own. They'll like you if you've built a rapport with them. Building rapport is all about demonstrating that you can put yourself in their shoes and see the world through their eyes, not just your own. You don't have to agree with them, but you do have to demonstrate that you've taken the trouble to understand them and can genuinely appreciate their views.

Speak to the Heart, and Not Just to the Mind

I once attended a "meet the presidential candidate" event for John Kerry at my neighbor's house. About two hundred people gathered around Mr. Kerry in the backyard as he held forth for about thirty minutes. Then he opened it up for questions. A woman raised her hand: "Mr. Kerry, you do such a good job of describing your thoughts logically, but when are you going to speak to our hearts, and do you actually think you can win the election if you don't?" I think we were all taken aback. But most of us knew what she meant. John Kerry's seeming inability to speak from the heart and to the heart may have cost him the election.

Many leaders think their audience wants logic, and they need to deliver logic, and logic alone. Nothing could be further from the truth. Human beings—the stuff audiences are made of—are physical, mental, and emotional. Address them holistically. I know it can be hard to speak *from* the heart and *to* the heart, but if you don't, you'll never be as effective as you could be.

How do you do it?

→ Talk about your dreams and aspirations, and talk about theirs, as well.

→ Don't just rely on logical constructs. Use stories, metaphors, and imagery. Storytelling is the most memorable form of communication. All great leaders, of virtually any type of organization, have been great storytellers. People listen to, are moved by, and remember stories much more than logical constructs.

→ Don't be afraid to let people know who you are and what you believe in.

I guarantee that if you look closely at all influential leaders in world history—whether you agree with them or not—*they described their dreams and aspirations to their constituencies.* They made good use of stories, metaphors, and imagery. And they were not afraid to show people who they were and what they believed in.

Tell Stories

This last one bears repeating: *tell stories!* Think about the most impressive and impactful leaders you can remember, and I will almost guarantee that they are excellent storytellers. Often, within a few days of having heard a speech, we've forgotten what it was about unless the speaker told a story. Sometimes, years later, we can remember the basic outline of the story. And remembering the basic outline of the story usually helps to remind us of the point that the speaker was trying to make. Stories are memorable.

In addition, they are interesting. How often, during a speech, do we find our minds wandering and our eyes glancing at our watches? Very often! Unless the speaker is telling a story! The point: The most effective leaders learn to make their points through stories. Learn to be a storyteller!

FINAL THOUGHTS

Finally, promising without delivering is unforgivable. Delivering without announcing is just plain stupid. If you're trying to impress someone, you might buy roses. Sending roses without a card, though, is a waste of money.

Some people have this view: "I told you when we got married that I loved you, I promised I'd tell you if I ever changed my mind, and I haven't changed my mind—so why do you want to know if I love you?!"

Think this makes for a successful marriage? It doesn't do much for leadership, either. If you don't like communicating, please don't aspire to lead. Leading is about communicating.

"The greatest tie of all is language," said Winston Churchill. "Words are the only things that last forever."[42]

---

42 Winston Churchill, "The Union of the English-Speaking Peoples" (from *"News of the World*, May 15, 1938), in *Churchill by Himself: In His Own Words* (New York City: Rosetta Books, 2013), 438.

Ask yourself:

→ How effective am I in communicating with my team, board, employees, clients, investors, regulators, government, and industry or community?

→ How effective are my team members in communicating with those same constituencies?

→ What could I do to become even more effective?

PART THREE

ACCOMPLISHING GREAT THINGS

Revolutionary Leadership

*"To this solemn resolution I came; I was free, and they should be free also;
I would make a home for them in the North, and the Lord helping me,
I would bring them all there."*
HARRIET TUBMAN

CHAPTER 7

IMPLEMENTING CHANGE

If You're Not Going Forward, You're Going Backward

This chapter talks about leading change. Few leaders can afford to operate indefinitely in a maintenance mode. Most leaders operate in a world of change, in which their organizations are required to change as well if they are to survive and prosper. Leading change is much more challenging than maintaining the status quo. There are at least four things to think about:

1. The importance of involving others from the start.

2. Anticipating, and preparing yourself for, resistance.

3. Insulating the changes you are targeting from the influence of the larger organization until they are strong enough to stand on their own.

4. In the end, making the change into everybody's success, not just the success of the people operating in the nucleus of the change.

*"I was the conductor of the Underground Railroad for eight years,
and I can say what most conductors can't say—
I never ran my train off the track and I never lost a passenger."*[43]

HARRIET TUBMAN

Best known for her work with the Underground Railroad, Harriet Tubman, an escaped slave, repeatedly risked her life returning to the South to transport another seventy to eighty slaves to freedom as far north as Canada. She inspired countless others to escape, as well. But Tubman's leadership and achievements extend far beyond this already extraordinary legacy. During the Civil War, she worked behind Confederate lines in South Carolina as a spy and scout for the Union Army. She led an armed military raid that liberated over seven hundred slaves. She worked in hospitals, providing care for soldiers and newly liberated slaves, including survivors of the 54th Massachusetts Infantry Regiment—the *"Glory"* regiment—after they led the attack on Fort Wagner. She helped John Brown plan his raid at Harper's Ferry. At great risk of recapture, she spoke at numerous antislavery and women's suffrage meetings. She raised funds for the freedmen's relief effort, providing education and assistance to liberated slaves. She raised money and bought land to establish a home for aged and infirm African Americans, where she spent her final years. She worked for decades to advance women's suffrage. Believed to have had temporal lobe epilepsy—the result of near-fatal head trauma while enslaved—Harriet Tubman refused to let adversity or other people's assumptions define her. She led by example through changing times, modeling courage, strength, compassion, creativity, and organizational genius. As the world changed around her—and because of her—she changed with it. Tubman constantly sought new ways to contribute, and she blazed her trail into an extraordinary legacy of leadership.[44]

---

43 Harriet Tubman, suffrage convention speech, New York, 1896, Harriet Tubman Historical Society website, accessed April 9, 2018, http://www.harriet-tubman.org.

44 Kate Clifford Larson, *Harriet Tubman: Portrait of an American Hero* (New York: A One World Book, published by The Random House Publishing Group, 2003).

Most of the leaders we think of as being among our best were leaders of change. George Washington led us from being a collection of British colonies to become a confederation of independent states. Abraham Lincoln led us from a country that was fracturing to one that was, at least on paper, reunited; and from a nation that endorsed the institution of slavery to one that abolished it. Gandhi led India from being a part of the British Empire to becoming an independent nation.

Harriet Tubman was equally involved in change, helping enslaved African Americans escape to become free people. Examples of leaders who are best known for implementing change are legion.

Many first-time leaders envision leading as "running" an organization. Integral to the idea of "running" an organization is the tacit belief that the leader's job is optimizing the success of the organization within the context of the *status quo*. In my experience, nothing could be further from the truth. The status quo is already history. The world is constantly changing. If you're not moving ahead, you're falling behind. If you are not consciously changing, you are losing ground. There is always something—a competitor, a megatrend, a new technology—that is threatening your ability to succeed and thereby maintain your place in the pecking order. As a leader, your job is not just to maintain your organization's ability to succeed within the context of the status quo. That task should be delegated to others. Far more, *your* job is to anticipate change, be it in the form of a clever competitor, a radically new technology, or an inevitable life-changing megatrend, and to initiate a response that will enable your organization to succeed in the future.

Great leaders are not stuck in the weeds, making day-to-day tactical decisions that are best left to their lieutenants. They are operating above the fray, focused on the future and on how to ensure that the organizations they lead are prepared to address the changes the future will inevitably bring. Or, in some cases, they are dissatisfied with their organization's current status within the existing status quo and are focused on changes they could usher in that would result in a better future for the people they are leading. This might be said of leaders like Moses or Harriet Tubman. In either case, they are focused on change: what changes are necessary, how to initiate these changes, and how to inspire others to help implement them.

In thinking about leading for change, there are at least four important things to consider:

1. Involving others from the start.

2. Anticipating resistance and preparing for it.

3. Protecting the agents of change from the influence of the organization as a whole.

4. In the end, when victory has been achieved, making the change everybody's success, not just the success of the agents of change.

INVOLVING OTHERS FROM THE START

The first rule of change management? Involve others! We must involve others in the process leading up to change-related decisions for two reasons: 1) our decisions will be better if we get input, and 2) people are more likely to support rather than sabotage if they're involved in the process.

When planning for change, it's always good to involve your boss (and if you're at the top, your board), your peers (if any), and your first lieutenants (direct reports), major stakeholders, and relevant experts in the process leading up to your decision. As I am sure you know, we do this for two reasons: 1) you will make better decisions, and 2) you will get the support of the people you involve.

That said, there will be cases, like a couple of the ones I have already discussed, where some of the first lieutenants, major stake-holders, and/or relevant experts, no matter how convincing the arguments or long and thorough the discussions, remain wedded to the status quo. (I would like to say "wedded to the past," because in the course of most lengthy discussions the status quo has already morphed into the past; yes, I have a bias for change.) As I discussed in prior chapters, after the discussions are over and the decision has been made, those who are still in disagreement have to decide: Will they stay and support the change, even though they are not yet convinced of its merit, or will they leave? There is no in between. Those who cannot support *must* leave.

ANTICIPATING RESISTANCE AND PREPARING FOR IT: Stages of Grieving

Even when you do your best to involve others in planning for change, you won't necessarily get support from the organization— at least not initially. Be prepared for that. If you're unprepared and don't have the courage of your convictions, you may be tempted to reverse your unpopular decision (and *all* decisions involving change are to some degree unpopular) before you've had a chance to figure out whether or not it was a good one. Most people not only react negatively to change, but they react negatively in a fairly predictable sequence. This phenomenon is analogous to grieving the loss of a loved one, as documented in *On Grief and Grieving: Finding the Meaning of Grief Through the Five Stages of Loss* by Elisabeth Kübler-Ross and David Kessler. As with grieving, the stages and their sequence are generally predictable.

Here's an example: At the start of the last recession, my management team met to decide how we would adjust our strategy to offset the downturn. We'd doubled the company's size in the two years prior and were basically on track to do the same in the next two years. But since the business cycle had turned and a recession seemed imminent, we knew we had to put on the brakes, at least as regards to hiring, or we'd tank ourselves over time. We decided to freeze headcount. Managers could replace, but not add. We were serious and swore a "blood oath" to support this decision.

Turning the plan into action, though, we met resistance. Had we not been resolved to support our decision, we might have reversed it. First, people pretended they hadn't heard us. When confronted, they said they weren't sure we'd actually said it because it was just too unbelievable. Once they realized it *was* real, some returned to their managers (my direct reports), saying they knew it was real, but were sure it didn't apply to them. Once they realized it *did* apply to them, they left, then returned again, trying to justify an exception. When they realized they couldn't justify an exception, they tried to find an acceptable end run—they tried to get around the rule with some kind of workaround. And when they realized there were no acceptable end runs, they left angry and decided they'd live with it, but they wouldn't be happy. This final stage lasts about six months to a year. After that, most people either conclude that it was the right decision after all, or they leave the organization. Knowing this predictable sequence of reactions may bolster your resolve.

THE LESSON FROM GENG ROAD

Here's another example of the "change curve." Our company's first CEO disliked having a headquarters because he thought it tainted employees with what he called "headquarters syndrome." Like Charlemagne, his throne traveled with him. Traveling from office to office, our headquarters was located wherever he was on any given day. (We had many small, widely dispersed offices to ensure proximity to the client.)

Our second CEO loved the idea of a headquarters. If possible, he would have eliminated all field offices and brought everyone back to headquarters. He loved the idea of having a veritable Versailles. He began closing the Northern California offices, pulling people back into our grand new headquarters building. One by one, the offices capitulated. But there was one holdout: the Palo Alto office on Geng Road. The Geng Road crowd found one reason after another to drag their feet. They all agreed: If we closed the Geng Road office and brought everyone back to headquarters, they'd all quit and their clients would leave us. They basically went through all the steps outlined earlier. Finally, the CEO had had enough. He "commanded" them to leave Geng Road and move to headquarters. They complied with a marvelous show of reluctance, swearing that they were right. They made it abundantly clear that, although *they* might not leave us immediately, our clients would, and they (both the employees and the clients) would never forgive us.

A few years later, I became CEO. Like our first CEO, I don't like having a headquarters. I believe that people at headquarters tend to spend too much time jockeying for position, engaging in toxic politics, and condescending to the people in smaller offices. Anyway, we had to be out in the market, near our clients, and therefore widely dispersed in smaller offices. One by one, I cajoled the client-facing people at headquarters to move into smaller offices closer to the clients—and one by one, they went. The holdout? The people slated to move into our newly leased office in Palo Alto, coincidentally on Geng Road. They found many reasons to drag their feet and they all agreed: If we moved them out of headquarters and back to Geng Road, they'd all quit and their clients would all leave us. They basically went through the same series of steps as before. But I was determined.

By the time I'd retired, they were all back on Geng Road. Now that I've retired, the new CEO will have decisions to make about office locations. Likely as not, he will want to return everyone to headquarters. And I will guarantee that the people on Geng Road in Palo Alto will be outraged.

If you're going to be in charge, you have to take other people's opinions into account. But you can't make your decisions based exclusively on the opinions of people reporting to you because any decision you make will involve change. And most people's instinctive reaction to change is that they don't like it. What I've observed is that when the CEO says, "I want to go right," everyone objects, and then they adjust.

SVB had offices all over the world, and we would frequently move people around. Often, the employee would be excited about the promotion, but the employee's spouse would object, saying, "No, we can't go there, it's a horrible place." A year later, once they were settled into the new location, they never wanted to leave.

In other words, you can't make decisions based exclusively on what people think. Everybody hates the status quo, but the minute you want to change it, everybody loves it. You can't be led by the masses, or you're not doing your job. People naturally resist change. I do, too. The only changes I like are the ones I decided on, and I don't like anybody else's. "Changes" are like pets and children: I like my own, but not necessarily yours.

Another example: The first person I remember firing was a totally deficient employee. She was not nice, not good at her job, and people complained about her constantly, asking each other when I was going to do something about her. Finally, I fired her. The backlash was enormous. "How could you do that?" everyone demanded. "We liked her so much!" Just remember, it's good to take people's thoughts into consideration, but you can't shy away from doing the right thing, or what you think is right, just because people will be against it.

No matter how good your decision is, you should count on people being against it. Don't go home and think, "Oh no, I've just made the worst decision of my life." If you did, it's probably because you acted too quickly and didn't get other people's opinions. But if you've thought it through carefully and solicited opinions, just expect that some (perhaps many) people will object. As a leader, you have to know when resistance is coming from everyone's natural human resistance to change and be able to factor that out of the equation. That's good judgment.

THE RULE OF THIRDS

A wise person once said that at any given time, a third of your employees will really like the direction you're taking them, a third will object, and the last third will be undecided, waiting to see what happens. If you devote your time to trying to convince the bottom third that objects, then the neutral middle third will gravitate toward the bottom third, to enjoy the same level of attention. Meanwhile, the top third will get discouraged because you're ignoring them. But if you devote your time and attention to the top third—the group of people who really like the direction you're taking them—the neutral middle third will join them, and the bottom third will either leave or gravitate toward the other two-thirds.

Leaders often devote their time to trying to make the unhappy people—the bottom third—happy. Example: It's time for the summer outing for a team of twelve to fifteen people (of course, a smart leader would assign this task to a committee). The group decides to go to the water park. A third of the people love water parks, a third hate them, and a third don't really care either way and are just waiting to see what happens. Many leaders would spend their time trying to assuage the hurt feelings of the bottom third who hate water parks. They would give the complainers a lot of oxygen. Instead, devote your time to the heroes, the people who are doing what you want them to do. That way, the middle-third group will think, "If I want to get a lot of praise and attention, I should go with that." The middle-third group will go with the people who are getting the oxygen. But if it seems cool to object, if the people who are complaining get all of your time and attention, the middle-third group will go with that. Everybody likes attention, and negative attention is often better than none at all.

Also, remember that some people just enjoy arguing. If you argue with them, they'll like it and want to keep it going. Don't waste your time.

PROTECTING THE AGENTS OF CHANGE FROM THE INFLUENCE OF THE ORGANIZATION AS A WHOLE

Most people are subconsciously wedded to the status quo. They may feel, at some level, that change is necessary. But, unless they have been appointed as agents of change, they are likely to at least subconsciously resist the change. I am not a psychologist, so I can only speculate as to why that is true. But I have observed it so many times that I am virtually certain it is true.

Example: Toward the end of my tenure as CEO of SVB, I came to the conclusion that we needed to revitalize our "private bank." Allow me to give you a little background. SVB has never been a retail bank; that is to say, we deal with companies, not with individuals. (In fact, our target market is even narrower than what I just said would imply. Today, we deal only with technology companies, venture capital firms, and a few hundred wineries.) Years ago, we started a small private bank whose purpose was to serve the needs of individual venture capitalists and corporate officers of technology companies (and wineries). For years, our private bank was very small. But, I could see that in the fifteen years that had intervened since we'd started the private bank, the competitive landscape had changed. A couple of other private banks had started to take an interest in the clients of our private bank—namely, the venture capital partners and the corporate officers of our tech companies (and wineries). I started to worry that, if these competitors were successful, they might over time start taking an interest in banking the corporate businesses that these wealthy individuals represented— namely, the tech companies and the venture capital funds themselves. In my view, the best defense was to expand and improve the product line and the personnel of our existing private bank in order to ward off these competitors.

For several months, I discussed this with key members of my board and key members of my executive management team. Over time, a number of them began to think that I was right. Once I'd convinced a few key ones, the others (in some cases reluctantly) followed. The next step was appointing some "agents of change." We put together a team of people representing the various relevant disciplines (compliance, legal, sales, product development, marketing, etc.) and "painted their faces with war paint." By that, I mean that we told them that this mission was an extremely important one, that the future of the bank depended on its success, and they would be handsomely rewarded if they were successful.

Then (and I will discuss this in the next chapter, "Leading for Innovation") we took the additional step of insulating this little team of "agents of change" from the rest of the organization for a year or more. We had to do this because the people who had not been chosen for this mission, at a subconscious level, I believe, all felt that it could not be done. They found numerous reasons to object. Their attitude was "cannot" rather than "can do." The same was true of the people who had not been chosen: the salespeople who had not been chosen, the product development people who had not been chosen, the marketing people who had not been chosen, etc. This was true across the board, notwithstanding the fact that an essential part of our culture has always been "supporting our co-workers," and that part of each person's bonus potential was based on the extent to which they did indeed support their co-workers.

In other words, we had to let the project proceed "under the protection of a bubble" for at least a year before we unveiled it and let it interface with the rest of the organization as it began to cultivate new customers with the benefit of its new and expanded product lines.

MAKE THE SUCCESS OF THE NEW INITIATIVE EVERYBODY'S SUCCESS, NOT JUST THE SUCCESS OF THE PEOPLE DIRECTLY INVOLVED IN THE CREATION OF THE NEW INITIATIVE

When the change (the new initiative) is complete and ready to implement, it is extremely important that it be celebrated. It is even more important that it be celebrated in a way that makes it clear that the success of the new initiative will accrue to the benefit of *everyone* in the organization, not just to the benefit of those directly involved.

Example: Near the beginning of my tenure as CEO, we made the decision to "go global." Here's what we meant by that: Technology is fundamentally a global industry, not a regional one. Most businesses, I believe, are regional. Take dairy farming, for example. Dairy farming is a regional business, not even a national one. Tastes, product lines, and accordingly, pricing, may vary across regions within a country. That said, technology is global. The iPhone is used around the world. You cannot be cutting edge in one country and not be cutting edge in all countries. Further, technology, being abstract, tends to cross borders, whether we want it to or not. The best technology will move from the area in which it was invented to all other areas over time, either legally or illegally. Finally, we all start each day with the same global knowledge base, and people around the world add to it every day, usually in small increments, sometimes in large ones, so that it is at least a little larger every night when we go to bed. Like it or not, in a certain way, it belongs to all of us.

As a result of this "logic," we came to the conclusion that we needed to be active in all the major innovation centers around the world, or we would slowly lose market share, even in markets in which our share was already large.

"Going global" is a dangerous undertaking. Many of our employees had already worked at other banks that had tried, and they knew how risky it is for a bank to try to establish a beachhead in another country. And only a few of our employees were themselves interested in becoming "agents of change." The desire to work "overseas" is unique to certain personality types. Not everyone is interested.

"Going global" is also expensive. Early on, the rumor got started that bonus checks throughout the company would be larger if we were not investing so much money in these global undertakings. To a certain extent that was true, at least in the short run. But, we were convinced that these investments were worth it. If we made them, in the (perhaps distant) future, bonus checks for everyone in the bank could be larger; and if we didn't make these investments, I, at least, was convinced that over time, bonus checks for everyone might be smaller.

So, our immediate challenge was convincing our troops, throughout the bank, that they would be better off in the future if we made the investment in "going global." We did our best. But it was always an uphill battle. For years, even after the global businesses were adding to our overall bonus pool, many people believed that they were subtracting instead. Over time, we "won" the "propaganda war," but it was difficult.

The lessons learned: To get everyone's support, you have to convince everyone that they (and not just the people immediately involved) will be better off. And you have to repeat the message, in various ways and in various contexts over time. Often, only after people have heard something many, many times will they come to believe that it is true.

Ask yourself:

→ How well do I perform in my role of leading change?

→ To what extent do I involve others in the process?

→ What aspects of leading change do I find frustrating or difficult?

→ How do I anticipate and handle resistance to change?

→ How well does my team perform its role in change management?

→ What could we do differently to improve our performance in this area?

"You can have no dominion greater or less than that over yourself."
LEONARDO DA VINCI

CHAPTER 8

LEADING FOR INNOVATION

What We Can Learn from Galileo

In this chapter, we'll talk about how to create an atmosphere in which the people in your organization are more likely to be creative:

1. What do we mean when we say "innovation"? The role of culture in encouraging creativity.

2. Elevate and prioritize good ideas.

3. The importance of war paint and courage.

4. Encourage trying out new approaches versus punishing failure.

5. Protect the innovators.

6. The importance of speed and the dread of red tape.

7. "Sharpen the saw."

8. Encourage individuality.

"Obstacles cannot bend me.
Every obstacle yields to effort . . .
He who fixes his course to a star changes not."[45]

LEONARDO DA VINCI

Scientist, inventor, painter, architect. Writer, mathematician, military engineer. Sculptor, anatomist, botanist, musician, civil engineer . . . what *didn't* Leonardo da Vinci do? Widely considered to be one of history's most innovative and talented thought leaders, da Vinci paved the way in a dazzling variety of fields. His intellectual curiosity drove him to advance humanity's state of knowledge; and he envisioned future machines, including tanks, helicopters, and bicycles. His "flying machine," based on a bat's physiology, is perhaps his best-known invention. Da Vinci's creativity and spirit of innovation have inspired change and invention over the centuries, and continue to have influence in our lives today.

People often ask me: "How do you lead in a way that helps to ensure innovation?" In today's world, organizations, corporations, and governments internationally are all asking the same question.

WHAT DO WE MEAN BY "INNOVATION"?:
The Nine-Dot Puzzle

One of the most overused clichés in business is "the nine-dot puzzle" or "thinking outside the box." In case you're not familiar with it:

---

45 Leonardo da Vinci, in Osvald Sirén, *Leonardo da Vinci: The Artist and the Man* (New Haven and London: Yale University Press, 1916), 230.

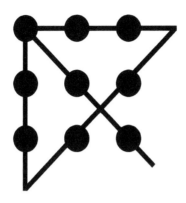

The concept is simple enough. You give someone a picture of nine dots (configured as in this picture but without the lines) and ask them to connect all nine dots, using no more than four straight lines, without lifting the pencil from the paper. The only way to do this is by going outside the imaginary square implied by the nine dots. Of course, most people fail because it never occurs to them (and you never told them) that they must, *and therefore may*, go outside the nine dots.

You can't turn a group of people with very little creativity into a bunch of creative geniuses simply by saying that it's necessary and okay to go outside the nine dots. The implication that you *can* is what's turned this whole idea into a cliché.

But you *can* create an organizational atmosphere that encourages people to go outside the nine dots, so to speak. Here's how:

1. Build a Culture in Which People Will Have the Courage to Speak Out

Build your culture along the lines described earlier in the chapter on "Building a Great Culture." This includes: 1) making sure that your organization functions more like an orchestra than a dogsled;

2) working to ensure that your team members interact with each other on an adult-to-adult basis (no passive-aggressive and no obnoxiously assertive people); 3) insisting on diversity while discouraging conformity; and 4) coaching managers to solicit the views of the people who report to them and listen in a way that ensures that their direct reports feel heard. This kind of culture does not ensure risk-taking, but it at least provides an atmosphere in which people will feel comfortable expressing themselves. People who feel comfortable expressing themselves are more likely to be willing to take risks.

Of particular note: This principle of creating an atmosphere in which people with good ideas feel comfortable expressing them *must* extend to the lowest level in the corporation. For two reasons: 1) so that people—at all levels—will feel respected, and 2) because lower-level people sometimes have ideas that are at least as good as (if not better than) those of the people at the top. Exactly *how* you go about soliciting ideas from lower-level people may vary from place to place and from time to time. I will leave that up to you; still, I strongly encourage you to try.

2. Develop a Mechanism for Selecting the Best Ideas from Among All the Ideas That Bubble Up

If you have done a good job of encouraging and including, great ideas will bubble up in greater numbers and faster than you can accommodate. You will need to develop a selection process, a method of deciding which ideas to pursue and which to postpone (sometimes indefinitely). A thorough treatment of exactly how to do that would take us into the area of project management, which is a separate discipline with a knowledge base all its own. Don't worry, if you need to go there, there are plenty of books on project management available.

That said, no matter what kind of selection process you decide on, consider the following. Your process will doubtless include a committee. When selecting the members of that committee, seven things are important: 1) The committee must represent all of the relevant disciplines; 2) no single discipline can dominate; 3) no single person may dominate; 4) the committee should include some lower-level people, not just higher-level people; 5) the people on the committee must be "glass half full" types, not "glass half empty" people; and 6) you should encourage them to make decisions with alacrity. Speed is of utmost importance.

Finally, number 7: Most such committees focus on the risk of doing something. Seldom do they focus on the risk of *not* doing something. To make good decisions, your committee must consider both. In my estimation, *more corporations have failed by not doing something than have failed by trying something new.*

I can imagine what you're thinking: A committee of the sort I just described sounds like a formula for disaster. But it's not. It's a formula for creativity. Remember, *you* are still in a position to veto any project that you feel is out of sync with your strategy, or just too risky. That said, if you want to be successful in addressing the future, I would recommend that you exercise your veto power sparingly.

If you don't try something, you will never know if it will work. If you do try something and it doesn't work, you can shut it down. And you will have raised the level of your organization's collective knowledge base.

3. Set Big Goals and Apply "War Paint"

Innovation means creating something new. That's a *big* goal to achieve. But what's most important is not just that innovation involves a big goal; what's most important here is that your employees and team members *perceive* their work as really and truly involving a big goal.

Ceremony is really important. And people love liturgy. When you're talking about vision, there's something reassuring to your audience about repetition—there's a reason this communication method has endured for over two thousand years. As a leader, it's important to incorporate storytelling and liturgy into every speech you make.

For years, two large paintings hung in my office. One showed a Native American warrior on horseback, galloping toward the viewer, spear in hand. I meant this to convey the need for courage, even ferocity, as a precondition for success. Be fierce!

For the first half of my career, I was basically a salesman, getting people to bank with us instead of somewhere else. That kind of work requires determination and courage. You have to become a warrior. Viewing your work in a way that lends a level of risk to it adds interest and meaning. To provide you with the motivation needed to maintain your determination, you will have to envision it as both noble and dangerous. If you're just trying to talk someone into taking your loan instead of another bank's loan, how meaningful is that? How fun is that? So in my mind, I would "demonize" my adversaries, knowing full well that it's not much fun to claim victory over a house cat—you want it to be a panther.

The second painting in my office showed a medicine man inside a teepee applying paint to a warrior's face, surrounded by other warriors waiting their turn in the ceremony. I meant for this painting to convey the basic human need of innovative people for big goals. The act of face painting signifies recognition on the part of the tribe that the warrior is taking on a *big* goal. That the mission on which we are sending him is both noble and dangerous.

If you're going to give people a mission, you need to include meaning and ceremony. You have to tell them how important it is. You can't just casually say, "Go into the forest and fight." You have to say, "The whole world will be better off if you do this." If people don't have a sense of importance and mission, they won't have the motivation.

Here's an example from corporate life: Years ago, I headed an office in Boston responsible for all of our bank's East Coast activities. At a certain point, we'd done enough business in Maryland that we felt justified in opening an office there as well. "Frank," I told the direct report I'd chosen, "I want to set up an office in Maryland, and I want you to lead it." To my great surprise, Frank showed almost no enthusiasm for the assignment. A few days later, he said, "I don't want the assignment."

"Why not?" I asked, shocked.

"I want to do something important."

"This *is* important."

"If that's true," Frank said, "then why aren't you acting like it is?"

After much discussion, I saw where I'd gone wrong. First, never assume that other people can read your mind. Second, nobody wants to take on a project, especially one that will disrupt their personal life (as moving to another state almost always does), if the chief—and therefore the rest of the tribe—doesn't think it's important. We signify our belief in the importance of a mission by applying "war paint" to the face of the appointed "warrior." I *should* have said at the outset: "Frank, our future depends on our expansion. Setting up an office for us in Maryland is an important mission, perhaps our most important one right now. There's only one person that I consider capable of taking on this project, and that's you! Our most important project right now depends on *you*. Will you please consider it, for me, for the office, for the bank?"

Consider what it's like to care for a loved one who is ill. The basic tasks are often unpleasant, and they're generally not interesting or particularly meaningful in isolation. But as part of the greater fabric of your relationship with that person, small acts like heating a bowl of soup or fluffing a pillow to give comfort take on significant meaning as part of your larger job in helping someone you care about, who needs you.

I know someone who doesn't really like any kind of work. When possible, I try to get him to turn it into a game. Work is inherently boring unless you turn it into something important—something with a mission, a sense of adventure, or greater meaning to it. It's really up to you. You can choose to be bored your whole life or you can choose to make things interesting.

People yearn for importance and meaning. Big goals provide that. If you want innovation, give your people big goals—and let them know that you consider them big as well.

Remember, virtually everyone wants to do something important. For the most part, if given the choice, people would rather be involved in a project that takes the organization forward, as opposed to a project that protects the organization from going backward. To attack is always much more fun than to defend. To encourage creativity, involve others when choosing which projects are most worthy and when executing them, and praise everyone who contributes, regardless of the outcome. If you are good at praising, I mean genuinely expressing gratitude and admiration, you will release a fountain of energy and motivation.

4. Praise Creativity, Avoid Criticizing Failure

I was having a cup of tea with a Western management consultant we once hired to work with our China team. "What's the most common problem you encounter in coaching management teams in China?" I asked.

Without hesitation, he said the most common problem is the patriarchal, dictatorial type of owner-operator who insists on making all the decisions and then criticizes his people for their lack of creativity.

If you want people to unleash their creativity, you must encourage and reward them for doing so. They need to know that you find unconventional answers interesting (like going outside the proverbial nine dots) and that you'll reward them for finding such answers. Rewards can include giving them "face," credit, money, etc.

What's most important is to consistently seek the opinions of those reporting to you. Marvel at their ideas. Don't judge them. Marveling rather than judging does *not* box you into implementing them. In the end, you—the leader—can decide which ideas to pursue. Even if you end up basing your decisions more on your thoughts than on opinions you've sought, find a way to give people credit for inspiring you.

Above all, never do to your employees what the Catholic Church did to Galileo. When he announced his discovery that the earth revolves around the sun (rather than the other way around), the Church tried him for heresy, found him guilty, forced him to recant, and sentenced him to house arrest for the rest of his life.

Not only did time and science prove the Church wrong on this front, the forced recantation had, of course, no effect on Galileo's understanding of or attitude toward the truth. As Galileo got to his feet after making his required abjuration, he reportedly muttered about the earth, *"Eppur, si muove."* ("Yet, it moves.")[46]

Being creative involves taking risks. Sometimes creative people will fail. Punishing them for failure will ensure that neither they nor their co-workers will continue trying to innovate.

Remember, don't look back, except to learn from your mistakes and the mistakes of others. Praise people for coming up with great ideas, even if they don't always work out. Praise people for executing great ideas, even if they don't always succeed. Focus on the future, and the people whom you are leading will as well.

In my first year as CEO, I decided to buy a mergers and acquisitions firm. I thought my reasoning was sound: The vast majority of our clients got acquired by somebody bigger, over time. When that happened, we lost a client. Why shouldn't we find some way of profiting from the sale of one of our clients to someone bigger instead? With that as our goal, we searched for an appropriate candidate. And we found one (or at least we thought we did). In the end, three years later, we had to throw in the towel. It didn't work. The reasons were many and would take too long to describe. In any case, we lost over one hundred million dollars. Many boards would have fired me. But not ours! Instead, they spent lots of time discussing the failure with me so that we would all understand what not to do next time. And then they praised me for my courage, and for the fact that we had all learned so much from the experience. In retrospect, I think that a lot of our progress since then is at least indirectly attributable to this learning experience. That said, had we had a less insightful board,

---

46 Galileo Galilei, "Eppur, Si Muove," in *Speeches That Changed the World: Over 100 of the Most Influential Speeches Ever Made* (New York: Metro Books, 2015), 80.

the bank might have ended up learning nothing, and I might have ended up without a job.

5. Protect the Innovators

By official accounts, when Steve Jobs wanted to advance Apple by innovating the Mac, he:

- Selected a small group to work on what would become the Mac.

- Told them how important the project was.

- Set them up in a separate building, physically removed from the existing facilities.

- Allowed them to plant a black pirate flag atop their new building.

- Refused entry to all but the new team.

- Gave them autonomy to innovate without interference.

- Gave them a deadline to enhance their sense of the task's importance.

- Avoided giving criticism, knowing they'd be their own worst critics.

I followed the same pattern years later when I decided (against most of my direct reports' judgment) to rehabilitate and radically reform our deteriorating private bank serving wealthy clients. Why? Because there's something in human nature—even in the best and most cooperative employees—that doesn't want projects to succeed unless they are personally involved. Perhaps it's like sibling rivalry. In any case, people often use all means at their disposal to sabotage. They'll find the project too risky, too likely to cannibalize existing products, too lacking in conformity to standards, too incapable of interfacing with existing systems, too expensive relative to expected revenues, etc., etc., etc. It's like a three-year-old who, when the parents aren't looking, mercilessly pinches the new baby.

Give your employees a big goal and the autonomy to achieve it without your interference, and they will innovate. Guaranteed!

From Leonardo da Vinci's dreams of flight to today's technology, the spirit of innovation continues to push the limits of what we thought possible. This spirit shone through in John F. Kennedy's words: "We choose to go to the moon. We choose to go to the moon in this decade and do the other things, not because they are easy, but because they are hard, because that goal will serve to organize and measure the best of our energies and skills, because that challenge is one that we are willing to accept, one we are unwilling to postpone, and one which we intend to win, and the others, too."[47]

And somewhere in all your hard work and creative thought, make sure that you and your team follow this advice from Leonardo da Vinci: "Every now and then go away, have a little relaxation, for when you come back to your work your judgment will be surer. Go some distance away because then the work appears smaller and more of it can be taken in at a glance and a lack of harmony and proportion is more readily seen."[48]

6. The Importance of Speed and the Dread of Red Tape

In the early 1990s, right after our first CEO left and our new CEO came on board, we went through an era in which our organization seemed to be obsessed with achieving consensus around every major decision before being willing to take action. As you might have already guessed, this tendency resulted in a very slow decision-making process. The emphasis was always on process, and seemingly never on

---

47 John F. Kennedy, *We Choose to Go to the Moon*, Address at Rice University, Houston, Texas, on September 12, 1962, USG-15-r29, National Archives and Records Administration, Office of Presidential Libraries, John F. Kennedy Library, accessed October 14, 2018, jfklibrary.org.

48 Leonardo da Vinci, from his *Notebook*, Quotations Book, accessed April 9, 2018, http://quotationsbook.com/quote/34276/.

outcome. For two reasons: First, it is impossible to achieve consensus whenever there is more than one person involved in making a decision. Some people are so indecisive that they cannot even achieve consensus when they are the *only* person involved. In order to justify holding out for consensus, people often defer making a decision under the pretense that they need more analysis. This is often just a pretense. As time rolls on, it becomes apparent that there is no such thing as enough analysis. The speed of progress comes to a slow grind as the organization waits for ever more analysis. Creative people are often less patient than those who are less creative. Accordingly, they either leave or—in discouragement—go underground.

The speed of our decision-making processes is an important factor in building an organization that encourages innovation. Slow decision-making drives out innovators. Remember, it is better to make a bad decision quickly than to take too long to make a good decision. It is possible to correct a bad decision. It is often impossible to regain the time you lost by being too late (or to rehire the innovators who left you in frustration).

7. Sharpen the Saw

There is a fable in China about "sharpening the saw." A woodcutter came into possession of a new saw, far better than his old one. It worked so well, in his first week using the new saw he cut down twenty trees. Oddly, in the second week, and working just as hard, he managed to cut down only fifteen, and in the third week, only ten. He couldn't figure out why. Then an older, wiser woodcutter told him: "You have to sharpen the saw every weekend." He tried it, and it worked. From then on, he consistently cut down twenty trees every week.

Encourage your employees to take time off, to "sharpen the saw." I believe that the average person can accomplish more in sixty hours than they can in ninety. And they are much more likely to be creative.

Our first CEO, Roger, regularly would disappear for an afternoon. We often wondered why and speculated as to what he might be doing. It turned out to be pretty simple. When Roger was trying to figure something out and found himself getting more and more tense without finding a solution, he'd just take the afternoon off and go to the movies. It relaxed him, and he knew that he found solutions more quickly when he was more relaxed.

8. China's Women's Soccer Team: "Steel Roses"

Today's China is obsessed with proving itself to the world. One way is through sports. Despite having devoted considerable resources to its women's soccer team, the team's results are not terribly impressive. According to Mark Dreyer, a British sports commentator in Beijing, the national teams are hampered by a "'military style system' of coaching and training that stifles individual skills, creativity, and even personality."[49] People will blossom if they are allowed to be the best version of who they really are, in all of their individual glory.

Ask yourself:

→ Have I built a culture that lays the groundwork for encouraging innovation?

→ Do I tell the people in my organization how important their work is to our mission? How can I include meaning and ceremony when giving people a mission?

→ Do I encourage and reward people in my organization for unleashing their creativity? Have I been guilty of the "Galileo Syndrome" at times?

→ Do I protect the innovators?

→ Are my people working more than is healthy? Are they too "burned-out" to innovate?

CROSS-CULTURAL LEADERSHIP

Leadership in a Flat World

"Hide your brilliance, bide your time."[49]

DENG XIAOPING

A TREMENDOUS OPPORTUNITY

In April 2011, I was scheduled to retire. I'd picked my successor far in advance, and although a few board members had—purely out of principle—pushed to consider outside candidates, most of the board members had long since embraced my choice. The transition was locked and loaded. I was scheduled to go home and play with the grandchildren.

For years, Ruth (my wife) and I had wanted to move to India for a year or two after I'd retired. We hoped the bank might find a role for

49 Deng Xiaoping, in Joanne Wallis and Andrew Carr, *Asia-Pacific Security: An Introduction* (Washington, DC: Georgetown University Press, 2016), 43.

us there as "statesmen." But as luck would have it, as the end of 2010 drew nearer, it became more and more apparent that the Indian regulators were still years from granting us a banking license. At the same time, however, the Chinese regulators were—miraculously— beginning to appear receptive to granting us a banking license. I say "miraculously" because getting a commercial banking license in China is a watershed event. Our bank was one of the first in known history to get one, and it took us years.

As the day of transition neared, the board began talking more about sending *me* to China. Ruth and I decided that if the opportunity became real, we would leap on it. What a tremendous opportunity at the end of one's career, to move to another country! Especially to a country like China that itself was in the midst of a watershed event: making the transition in record time from a third-world backwater to the fastest-growing and potentially largest economy in the world. A chance to live in China, a country that has fascinated Americans of all ilks since our first encounter in 1784! We both felt this opportunity was too good to pass up. We would *have* to go!

So, in May 2011, just a few weeks after passing the baton to Greg, we moved to Shanghai!

We stayed for nearly four years. In retrospect, those years were hands-down the most interesting of our adult lives. We found life in China to be totally, 100 percent engaging. To spend every single day in this uniquely distinctive environment, learning about a culture and a system so different from our own, imbued us with a radically heightened sense of being alive, and (largely I think in our imaginations) with a profound sense of "clear and present danger." Chinese culture, Chinese history, Chinese language: What could be more challenging? Or more *interesting*!

At the same time, what could be more *frustrating*? Besides the usual challenges of learning to navigate a totally new and radically different environment, the Chinese system presented us (especially me, trying to build a bank) with challenges I never could have imagined before our arrival.

So, as a springboard to my humble attempt to shed light on the topic at hand, "cross-cultural leadership," I'd like to describe a few of the (for us, at least) surprising occurrences of our first several months in China.

Shortly after our arrival, I contacted my counterpart at the Shanghai Pudong Development Bank (SPDB). The Shanghai government had selected SPDB to be our joint-venture partner. If you want to enter into the banking business in China, of course, you need a banking license, as is required in most countries, but—in addition—you need a joint-venture partner. Ostensibly this is to protect *you* from the risk of doing business in a market as different from most Western markets as is China's. That said, it also offers the joint-venture partner an opportunity to learn your business model without having to pay tuition.

Mr. Zhang, the (now) former president of SPDB, was to be the chairman and I was to be the president of the new bank. At the time, I was not aware that in China the chairman goes to work every day and acts as a CEO would in the United States. The president reports to the chairman and acts as a COO would in the United States. It took me a few months to figure out that Mr. Zhang had the Chinese model in mind, not the US one.

We hadn't received our license yet; in fact, it didn't arrive until October of that first year in China. I suggested that we form a working group to prepare for the day when the license would arrive. Mr. Zhang thought that was a good idea, but for some inexplicable reason, he kept postponing appointing people from SPDB to the working group. Meanwhile, our appointees on the SVB side were all lined up and ready to go.

While he seemingly capriciously postponed appointing people from his side to the working group, Mr. Zhang proposed that I spend my time working on the eventual org chart. So, I did. Mr. Zhang and I ended up playing an extended version of "pin the tail on the donkey." Mr. Zhang didn't like any of the various iterations that I proposed, but he was either unwilling or unable to describe to me what was, in his view, missing. Eventually, it came out: Mr. Zhang wanted to see a "general office," and I hadn't provided for one. Long story short, the "general office" is a Chinese convention that goes back to dynastic times. The general office was a buffer between the emperor (or, today, the party secretary) and the rest of the world. Today, any communications between the party secretary and the rest of the world are filtered through the general office staff. It affords "protection" in both directions. On the one hand, nothing can come in without going through the filter of the general office. On the other hand, nothing can go out, either. This latter feature helps to ensure that party secretaries don't go rogue. They all read from the same script, and the general office helps to ensure that.

Only later did I figure out why it was taking Mr. Zhang so long to appoint his people to the working group. Even as president of SPDB, Mr. Zhang did not have the power to appoint. Appointments are all handled by the party committee (at the bank), which in turn is responsible to the Organization Department, a national institution. In short, there are essentially three overlapping organizations in a situation like the one in which I had just become involved. Nobody explained this to me before I got there. I just had to figure it out. There is the Party, which is the highest authority, yet always works behind the scenes, and for all practical purposes is invisible to someone like me. Then there is the government, in this case, the Shanghai government, which owns SPDB (virtually all banks in China are owned by government entities). The Party controls the government, but from behind the scenes. Finally, there is the bank itself. Mr. Zhang is the president, and he reports to both the chairman (Chairman Ji) and the Party Committee. He's primarily an executor, not a decider. In particular, he does not make appointments; the Party Committee does. In its own good time.

Part of this I learned through a chance experience involving a Mr. Gao, known to us as Thomas. After the license arrived in October, and Mr. Zhang was able to announce the Party Committee's appointees to the working group, Thomas was among them. He'd been selected by the Party Committee because he was in charge of a department within SPDB responsible for monitoring all of the joint ventures in which SPDB was involved. I decided to take Thomas to lunch to get to know him and see what I could learn. Thomas was, to say the least, pompous, and fully cognizant of the superior position that SPDB occupied within the construct of our joint venture. Over lunch, Thomas told me about the Party Committee. He warned me that I would never know who they were or what they had decided, but he was their representative, and he had been sent to watch me and to make sure that I didn't mess up. All important decisions, Thomas assured me, would be made by the Party Committee, not management and not the board. Afterward, I asked Mr. Zhang about what Thomas had told me. Both Mr. Zhang and his "first lieutenant," Mr. Li, told me to ignore Thomas. He just made these things up, they said. As it turned out, both Thomas on the one hand, *and* Messrs. Zhang and Li were right. Reality (I think, although I am not quite sure) turned out to be a combination of the two descriptions.

Once the working group was able to swing into action in the late fall of 2011, we became almost immediately engrossed in three other issues: the logo, the computer system, and the location of the new bank.

Regarding the logo, earlier in the process, when we were "dating" our future joint-venture (JV) partner, in the 2009–2010 timeframe, all of us (myself; my future successor as CEO of SVB, Greg; Mr. Li; and Mr. Zhang) had been in agreement: *The JV was to be an independent entity.* We (SVB and SPDB) were the parents, and the JV (later to be named SSVB, meaning Shanghai Silicon Valley Bank) was the offspring. Both parents vowed never to compete against the joint venture.

That said, when it came time to decide on a logo, SPDB wanted our offspring to use their SPDB logo as if it were a division of Mr. Zhang's side. I wanted it to have its own logo. We argued and argued. Mr. Li invited me to a meeting with SPDB's head of marketing, Ms. Hong, who reported to him. She lectured me for over an hour in an oppressively condescending way on all the reasons why the JV should use SPDB's logo. I wouldn't budge. Finally, Mr. Zhang capitulated. To make it easier for him to capitulate, I asked him if he would design the logo himself with the help of a design firm. He did, and we used it, and still do to this day.

The second bone of contention to be addressed by the working group was the computer system. What would we use for an IT backbone? As expected at this point, SPDB wanted us to use theirs. The problem with that was, we felt, obvious. SPDB's IT backbone was "homegrown." Modifying it to accommodate the needs of the joint venture was extremely difficult, if not borderline impossible. This topic was less emotionally charged, and in the end, we purchased a system from Oracle.

The most emotionally charged issue was the office location. In China, it's often the case that "like" businesses congregate together. For example, there's an entire street in Shanghai in which every shop sells office supplies, another in which every shop sells musical instruments, etc. Most of the banks register in the newest district that was established for this very purpose about thirty years ago on the other side of the river: Pudong (meaning "east of the river"). Today, the beautiful skyline featured in every tourist brochure describing Shanghai is the skyline in Pudong, viewed from the original (western) side of the river.

Nearly four hundred financial institutions are registered in Pudong. Mr. Zhang insisted that our bank locate in Pudong because *all* banks do. But I wanted our bank to be in Xintiandi, an area in the Huangpu District, west of the river, that had been developed around the same time as Pudong by the famous Hong Kong developer Vincent Lo. The difference is that Xintiandi is "cool" and Pudong isn't. SVB has always tried to locate in areas that are "cool," or at least perceived as such by entrepreneurs, who are largely younger and more "disruptive." So, for weeks Mr. Zhang and I argued. I'd say Xintiandi, he'd fire back Pudong. Little did we know that Mr. Chen, the former party secretary of the Yangpu District, an older industrial area that was trying to transform itself into an "innovation center," was lobbying the Shanghai government behind our backs.

In the end, neither Mr. Zhang nor I prevailed. In China, the government decides where you will locate your bank. We are now the only bank in Shanghai located in Yangpu, and probably always will be.

Later, when we started designing the space for our new bank in Yangpu, the government gave us a favorable lease rate in a brand-new building not far from Siemens. We had two entire floors. To lead the project, Mr. Zhang chose Mr. Shen, who had been selected by the SPDB Party Committee to be the head of our general office. When the architects were far enough along, Mr. Shen showed me the floor plan. I could barely believe my eyes: Mr. Zhang's office was identical to mine, and in combination, they took up about 40 percent of one of the two floors. Not only that—each of our offices was comprised of two rooms: one with a desk and one with a bed. "Why the bed?" I asked. Mr. Shen explained that in times gone by, everybody took a nap after lunch, at least in summer, due to the heat in Shanghai. The top guy(s) always had a room with a bed, and all of the others just put their heads down on their desks for about thirty to forty-five minutes. "Do they still?" I asked. Not so much, Mr. Shen told me, but many presidents, especially in banking, still hang on to their beds. I told him I thought we should dispense with the bedrooms in the interest of economy.

My next surprise came a few months later, in 2012. I was invited to speak at a conference, held by the government, on how to provide banking services to tech companies. As it turns out, *virtually all* conferences on any aspect of banking are held by the government. First, all banks are owned by the government; and second, any assembly of people has to be approved by the government. I arrived a little early, found my seat in the reserved section in the front, and settled in. A few minutes later I felt a tap on my shoulder. It was Mr. Ge, an officer from SPDB and one of our JV board members, sitting next to me. He, too, was going to give a speech on banking tech companies. I was surprised, to say the least. First of all, both parents had vowed not to compete against the offspring, so—logically—SPDB shouldn't have had a department addressing the needs of tech companies. And second, Mr. Ge seemed to me to be one of the least knowledgeable bankers—with respect to working with tech companies—in all of China. When it came his turn to speak, Mr. Ge marched to the podium and clicked on his first slide. I almost fell out of my chair. It was one of the slides we had used only a few weeks prior in a presentation we had made to the officers of SPDB to help them understand our business model. And so were the rest of his slides. After his short speech, Mr. Ge returned to his seat beside me, tapped me on the shoulder, and, grinning like a schoolboy who'd just gotten his first A, asked me: "How'd I do?"

You may be asking yourself, why were we teaching the officers of SPDB our business model? A month or two before, Mr. Zhang had asked me to come see him. He had something he wanted to discuss. When I arrived, I was surprised to see Mr. Zhang looking so unhappy. He was very disappointed, he said, to discover that we (the SVB contingent) were withholding information that would help them (the SPDB contingent) understand their investment. When I asked what on earth he was referring to, he replied, "The algorithm." We had an algorithm, he insisted, and we were not disclosing it. I didn't know whether to laugh or cry. SVB does *not* have an algorithm. At first, I was baffled. Then it occurred to me:

Wells Fargo is reputed to have an algorithm to automate lending to very small businesses, like dry cleaners or small retailers. But we do not. Lending to start-up tech companies is very risky and very complicated. Whereas Wells depends on relatively modestly paid, somewhat less experienced people to lend to very small businesses, SVB relies on relatively experienced, well-paid bankers to lend to technology start-ups. For Wells, it's a science; for SVB it's an art. SVB *does not* have an algorithm. So, to "regain our credibility," we gave a presentation to all of SPBD's senior officers and explained our business model. And we used the same slides that found their way into Mr. Ge's speech a few months later.

Finally, in October 2011, the Chinese banking regulator, the CBRC, granted us our banking license. We were elated. But we were not so thrilled to learn that our license granted us permission to do one thing and one thing only: to open our doors. It turns out, that's all a banking license in China grants you permission to do. Taking deposits requires another, separate license, making term loans yet another, making working capital loans another, exchanging money another, etc. Even setting up a website that lets customers view their accounts online requires a separate license, and you can't even apply for that particular license until you've been in business for one year. The application process for each of these licenses requires months, if not years. We're now eight or nine years into it, and we still don't have all the licenses we need.

The worst surprise? We weren't allowed to use Chinese currency for three years. According to a long-standing law at that time, a brand-new bank in China with any element of foreign ownership could not use Chinese currency for its first three years of operations.

This was for our own good, the CBRC (the banking regulator in China) assured us. By precluding us from doing much, the rule helped us, they said, because China is so different and the Chinese market so risky, that applying the brakes for the first three years would give us a chance to learn more about the market. When we could finally use Chinese currency, we'd be less likely to get ourselves into trouble.

In the meantime, the CBRC encouraged us to do what all good people in China do: Help China develop. We could do so, they said, by teaching other Chinese banks our business model.

Let's pause a moment to reflect. How would you have felt, at this point, had you been in my shoes? What would you have thought? Most important, what kind of theory about how China operates would you have developed to explain to yourself all you'd experienced?

My advice to anyone in a similar situation, from today's vantage point: *Withhold judgment.* Record your experiences so you can refer to them later. At the same time, try hard to withhold judgment. At least until you learn more.

Better yet, develop a working hypothesis. Test it daily, both with real-world experience and with study. Study can take the form of reading. During our four years in China, Ruth and I each read over fifty books on Chinese history, Chinese culture, and doing business in China. Supplement your reading with personal interviews. I went out of my way to seek out "Old China Hands" (Westerners who had been doing business in China for many years) and to interview them, take notes on what they said, and then reread and reflect on my notes later. I also went out of my way to meet as many knowledgeable people as I could, both Chinese and expats, and ask them questions. Finally, supplement your reading and interviewing with experience. Take notes on everything that seems relevant. Relentlessly iterate: In light of what you've learned, revise/update your working hypothesis. And keep a record of your iterations.

I also found it useful to set up an advisory board. I set it up in Beijing, out of our market at that point in time, to keep it somewhat secret (although I've come to believe that Westerners have no secrets in China). I populated it with a small number of very select Chinese businesspeople whom I believed I could trust (and still do). Unlike most advisory boards, which are really marketing arms in disguise, I asked for advice—real advice—on topics that were often somewhat sensitive. In doing so, I made myself vulnerable, but in the end, it was worth it. The advisory board was often very critical of the things I had done. But their advice saved me, I believe, from *really* failing.

Finally, I spent a great deal of time seeking feedback from trusted advisors in Shanghai. Even more important, I used that feedback to examine my filter. Each of us has at least two filters: one governing what we hear and one governing what we say.

What do I mean by that? At the most superficial level, when I say "house," what do I envision? When my conversation partner hears the word "house," what does he envision?" Often these are two totally different things.

At a deeper level, when I use analogies intuitive to most Americans, are my Chinese audiences "getting them"? They may smile and nod (I found that Chinese employees are often very good smilers and nodders), but do they really know what I mean? For instance, many Americans love sports analogies. Do Chinese audiences even know what sport you're referring to, much less how it works? I'm not really into sports, so my analogies tend to be historical ones. When I talk about encouraging a group of people who are struggling through a difficult time (for example, waiting three years to use Chinese currency), I'm likely to reference Moses leading the Hebrews through the desert for thirty years to the promised land. Does my audience even know who Moses is? If not, why are they all smiling and nodding? In China, my counterpart might make reference to Mao's "Long March" instead.

I am profoundly impressed by the extent to which language informs our perceptions. For example, if you ever took Linguistics 101, you may recall that Eskimos have thirteen or fourteen words for snow because in their perception, there are thirteen or fourteen different kinds, and which kind they're dealing with can make a practical difference. In English, we have about four: snow, powder, slush, ice. As it turns out, my conversation partners at SPDB are all: 1) members of the Chinese Communist Party, 2) de facto members of the Shanghai government, and 3) officers at SPDB. Astoundingly, my Chinese business partners didn't differentiate between the three to the extent that I do. It takes many Americans years before they realize that Party, government, and business are often all the same thing in China. Many Americans consistently divide the people they meet and the experiences they have with them into separate categories: business, and government, and Party. They don't realize that to the people they're dealing with, *business, government, and Party may be the same, not three different things.* So what? you may ask. Well, this failure to realize that Party, government, and business are often the same thing can lead many Western leaders to downplay the importance of "government relations" when they go to China. They tend to think: "If we just obey the laws and stay out of trouble, we don't really need to interface with government or Party. Anyway, even if we do, we should give that responsibility to our least expensive resources. Why spend money on something we're not even sure is necessary?" It may take these leaders years (lost years) to finally discover that the government controls business in ways that are unheard of in the United States and that failing to develop relationships with relevant government entities *is to do so at your peril.*

My entire "theory of China" would require more pages than you're probably willing to read, so let me content myself with just a few examples:

First, our respective negotiation styles. Many, if not most, of us in my age bracket were to one degree or another schooled in the Harvard Negotiation Project's famous book, *Getting to Yes*. We are constantly seeking mutual ground. Chinese negotiators typically are not. Consciously or otherwise, they are schooled in *The Art of War*, the negotiation and military manual written about 2,500 years ago by Sun Tzu. These respective styles are *totally* different. The differences can lead the American side to believe that the Chinese cannot be trusted, and the Chinese side to believe that the Americans are either patsies or—ironically—that *they* cannot be trusted.

A second example: Chinese society is, on average, much more hierarchal than ours in the United States. People in China tend to respect authority because it is authority. People in China don't generally send bad news up the ladder to the top. If you're running a company in China, don't expect to hear bad news from the people who report to you. You'll have to develop some other mechanism for discovering bad news, assuming there is any. If you listen closely to your Chinese employees, and if you take what they say at face value, you may conclude that you walk on water (another of my Western analogies). Trust me, you don't, and you most certainly do not in China.

A third example: People in China are less inclined to "stick out" than Americans. In general, they will deflect praise. If you say, "I want to commend Pei Ke for the excellent job that she did," and then give her a chance to respond, she'll begin with, "I couldn't have done it without the leadership of Ken and the support of my team." Pei Ke wants to blend in. Of course, she loves the praise, but she still wants to blend in. She's reluctant to appear different, even if different—as is true in this case—means better. In general, Chinese people seek strength in unity. If you're from Silicon Valley, for example, you might say that Americans seek strength in diversity. In China, unity—not diversity—is a virtue.

If you're planning to lead an organization in China, in which *both* Chinese *and* Americans will be working together, my best recommendation is this: given that your culture and filters are *so* different from those of your Chinese counterparts, try your best to build a new, third, *shared* culture over the long haul.

There's no better way of bringing together people from different cultures than shared experiences: activities, outings, discussions, etc. Invite your counterparts to create with you a new, third, *shared* culture over time. Start from scratch, not from the springboard of either your culture or theirs. Work together on it. Don't ask one side or the other to come up with a straw man; instead, start with a "blank sheet of paper," so to speak. This can be a long, laborious process, but keep at it.

Challenge each other to expound on the meaning of concepts that are dear to them. You may find, as I often did, that we thought we were talking about the same thing, when in fact, we were not.

Over-communicate. Much of your work will be done in smaller groups, given that research shows that the optimal size for a discussion group is approximately eight people. When a group has a result to share, share it widely, expansively, and often.

Make sure both groups, Chinese *and* Americans, have responsibilities. Often, it will appear to the Chinese that the Americans are the overlords and that the Chinese are being relegated to a secondary position. Don't let that happen. Make sure there is balance. Make sure that the Chinese side does not and cannot feel subordinate.

Compromise, or let each side win from time to time: perhaps with respect to different issues, and always in a balanced fashion. Both sides will tend to think that their way of doing things is superior. Make sure that both sides feel superior, at different points in time. For example, we ran into a project management issue that threatened to mushroom into a much bigger problem if we hadn't taken steps to mitigate it. Specifically, our project manager was American, and the project team was Chinese. The project was one of the most difficult of all: installing and rendering functional the IT backbone provided by Oracle. Basically, the American project manager wanted to spend months planning even the minutest detail, and only then to begin executing those plans. The Chinese team wanted to plan out the next three to four weeks' work, then work those plans, then plan again, for the next three to four weeks' work. It almost came to an insurrection. In the end, we opted to send the American project manager home and go with the Chinese approach. For the Chinese team, it worked out better, both in terms of outcome and in terms of how they felt about the process.

Finally, if you take your business to China, make it look and act like a Chinese company. The way customers perceive and interact with products; the way the distribution systems function; the way the social, legal, and regulatory systems work—in China, these are all Chinese. If you try to superimpose the American counterparts, you will fail. Localization is a many-faceted, many-layered phenomenon. Take all the time you will need investigating and querying to discover exactly what might constitute localization in every given instance. Most Western failures in China are traceable to a failure to localize to the extent necessary to succeed in China.

Ultimately, that will mean having Chinese management in charge. Three times I was invited to speak at the Party School in Beijing. This is the school for advanced management training for members of the Chinese Communist Party. Three times I spoke, and three times I received the same enthusiastic response. The audience loved what I said. They loved our bank. So much so, they said, that they wanted to have one of their own. Three times I said to them: "You *do* have one of your own. We are it! 99 percent of our employees are Chinese citizens, 100 percent of our clients are registered Chinese companies. The Chinese government owns 50 percent of our stock. This is *your* bank." And three times they responded by saying: "Yes, yes, we know, we know, *but we want one of our own!*"

Success, if it's even possible, will come from patience, taking the long view, intense over-communication, empathy, willingness to compromise, and—ultimately—becoming Chinese.

At the same time, we must always seek to avoid being taken advantage of and to never take advantage of others.

My conclusion: I'm not yet prepared to make any generalizations about how to lead in China. Like many Westerners, the more time I spend in China, the less comfortable I am making generalizations. That said, I am convinced that China and the US are different enough that a guide to leading an organization in China would have to be different from one intended for use in the US.

Sadly, most Western businesses that venture forth into China do so without having spent enough time learning about the hidden yet vast differences between Western and Chinese cultures.

Further, I am convinced that *the age of globalization has only just begun*. Yes, globalization has in the very recent past engendered backlash, and justifiably so. That said, this backlash will not bring it to an end. It will most certainly continue, at an increased rate. I say this for the following reasons: First, our world is arguably too small to accommodate the roughly eight billion people inhabiting it today. Viable living space is too small; and accessible resources, such as water, are too few. We keep bumping into each other, as would too many people living in too small an apartment. This requires communications and "rules of the road" for getting along with each other, and that spells globalization.

Second, too many of our most significant and pressing problems are global in nature. They cannot be solved unless and until we all, in particular the US and China, learn to work together effectively.

Third, global supply chains, and in particular those involving the US and China, are so intertwined that it would be very difficult if not almost impossible to tease them apart again.

Fourth, unless and until standards of living are more or less equal around the world, businesses will travel the globe seeking lower costs. This has been true since technology began to make traveling the globe economically feasible. It will continue, and, again, at an ever-increasing pace, thanks to the technology that enables it.

Finally, notwithstanding the current animosity in many countries toward immigrants, people enjoy and desire diversity. As soon as China began to get rich after the death of Mao, those Chinese who could, driven by curiosity and a fascination with differences, began to travel the globe, just to see what was out there. That will not stop soon. Curiosity is a natural human drive. And, for those of us who live and work in Silicon Valley, diversity has proven to be a major benefit. I believe that a handful of Chinese and a handful of Westerners, working together, can solve problems better and faster than either of those groups could working alone.

In short, the need to learn how to manage people and projects in a global world will only intensify. We have no choice but to learn.

Ask yourself:

→ When speaking to an audience from another culture or country, am I using stories, analogies, and examples that will be clear to them?

→ When negotiating with people from another culture or country, do I understand the potential cultural differences in negotiating style?

→ When working with a cross-cultural team, do I make sure that both groups have responsibilities and that both "win" on a fairly even basis?

→ Do I understand the importance of compromise when working with a cross-cultural team?

→ Long before I am ready to leave or retire from my leadership position, have I identified and groomed one or more possible successors, (i.e., good inside candidates)?

ABOUT THE AUTHOR

Ken Wilcox currently serves as Emeritus Chairman of Silicon Valley Bank and was both President and Vice Chairman of SPD Silicon Valley Bank, Silicon Valley Bank's joint-venture bank in Shanghai.

Mr. Wilcox was previously the CEO of SVB Financial Group. In that role, he successfully pursued a strategy of expansion and diversification, while remaining focused on the group's core niches of technology, life sciences, venture capital, and premium wineries.

Mr. Wilcox is a member of the Board of the Asia Society of Northern California, Treasurer of the Asian Art Museum, and a member of the 21st Century China Center Advisory Board. He is also the Chief Credit Officer of Columbia Lake Venture Debt Fund, an adjunct professor and member of the International Advisory Board at Fudan University in Shanghai, and an advisor to a number of start-ups. From 2006 to 2012, Mr. Wilcox was a member of the board of directors of the Federal Reserve Bank of San Francisco.

In 2008, Mr. Wilcox was named "Banker of the Year" by *American Banker*. He earned the distinction of "Entrepreneur of the Year" by

Ernst & Young in 2009 and 2010. The Yangpu District of Shanghai has also honored Mr. Wilcox with an "Innovation Contributor Award." In 2013, the Shanghai Municipal Government presented Mr. Wilcox with the "Magnolia Silver Award," a municipal honor given to expatriates for their outstanding contribution to the city's economic, social, or cultural development.

Mr. Wilcox earned a master's degree in business administration from Harvard Business School, as well as a PhD in German studies from Ohio State University. Mr. Wilcox can be reached at redmga56@gmail.com.

Citations for captions on pages 28, 84, 98, 156, 170.

Page 28:

"Do I not destroy my enemies when I make them my friends?"

Abraham Lincoln, quoted in Martin Luther King Jr's "Sermon 5: Loving Your Enemies," *Strength to Love* (New York: Harper & Row, 1963), page 39, accessed June 8, 2021, https://quoteinvestigator/2020/05/13/make-friends/.

Page 84:

"Courage! Do not fall back; in a little the place will be yours."

Joan of Arc, quoted in Willard Trask, comp., trans., *Joan of Arc: Self-Portrait* (New York: Collier Books, 1961).

Page 98:

"Diversity in counsel, unity in command."

Cyrus the Great, Goodreads, accessed June 18, 2018, https://www.goodreads.com.

Page 156:

"To this solemn resolution I came; I was free, and they should be free also; I would make a home for them in the North, and the Lord helping me, I would bring them all there."

Harriet Tubman, quoted in Sarah Hopkins Bradford, *Harriet, The Moses of Her People* (1886), accessed June 8, 2021, https://en.wikiquote.org/wiki/Harriet_Tubman.

Page 170:

"You can have no dominion greater or less than that over yourself."

Leonardo da Vinci, "maxim 1192," *The Notebooks of Leonardo da Vinci, Complete* (Project Gutenberg, 2004), accessed June 8, 2021, https://www.gutenberg.org/cache/epub/5000/pg5000.html.

CPSIA information can be obtained
at www.ICGtesting.com
Printed in the USA
LVHW010008141022
730615LV00008B/368

9 781949 003352